THE BACHELOR H. J. O'Rourke is the best-
selling author of *Modern Manners, Republican Party
Reptile, Holidays in Hell, Parliament of Whores, Give War
a Chance* and *All the Trouble in the World*. He writes for
Rolling Stone and lives in New Hampshire and
Washington, D.C.

The Bachelor Home Companion

Camus had it all wrong about the myth of Sisyphus— it's not symbolic of life, just housekeeping.

THE
BACHELOR
HOME
COMPANION

A Practical Guide to
Keeping House Like a Pig

BY P. J. O'ROURKE

Photographs by Alan Rose

PICADOR

To Alma

who cleaned my house and straightened my life,

for nearly ten years and without whom everything in this book

would have been true.

First published 1987 by Pocket Books, a division of the
Atlantic Monthly Press, Inc., New York, and simultaneously in Canada

First published in Great Britain 1993 by Picador
an imprint of Macmillan General Books
Cavaye Place London SW10 9PG
and Basingstoke

Associated companies throughout the world

ISBN 0 330 33175 2

7 9 8 6

A CIP catalogue record for this book is available from
the British Library

Printed and bound in Great Britain by
Cox & Wyman Ltd, Reading, Berkshire

ACKNOWLEDGMENTS

$\mathcal{T}$he Introduction, chapter 9 and parts of chapter 7 originally appeared, in somewhat different form, in *Parade* magazine. The author thanks Walter Anderson, editor of *Parade,* for proposing the subject of bachelor housekeeping, and Elaine Kaufman, proprietor of Elaine's restaurant, for insisting the *Parade* articles be turned into a book.

Further thanks are due to Jean McBride, who suggested the coffee-cup ring on the title page; Tom Yellvington for his recommended use of spray deodorant on dirty socks and his Egg Foo Breakfast recipe; Michael Nesmith for telling the author about the Bill Martin dishwashing method; Bill Martin for inventing that method; Brock Yates, retired bachelor, for his observations on "the four unmarried-male food groups"; Larry Gray for the "floaters" recipe; Chris Isham for inventing Doggy Melts; Gerry Sussman for the phrase "death over easy"; Debbie Babson for her Girlfriend Chicken recipe; Debbie Babson, again, and Rob

Stephenson for founding BARK (Bachelors Against Rude Kids); Winston Groom for his recipe for horrible wild ducks; Mike Burke for discovering that you can heat canned food by sticking it into the air cleaner on a car engine; Constance Bosworth for her extensive help on the Bachelor Cooking chapters, and for being adorable and for hardly squealing at all when the author kept a Jell-O mold with a dead mouse in it in his refrigerator for two weeks; Ronald E. Burr for his underwear washing tip; Britain Hill for her photo ideas and suggestions; Evelien Bachrach, Matthew Seeger, Virginia and Peter Russell, Rob Stephenson, William V. Bowers, Lauranne Shea, Trisha Cassetta, Court Barrett, Anne Diebold, and Anne Rose for their kind services as photo models; Christopher and Claire Bean and their children, Andy and Katie, for photo model services above and beyond the call of duty; the Beans and William and Carol Bowers for providing photo locations; Dan and Ann Griffin, owners of Soap and Suds in Jaffrey, New Hampshire, for letting us disrupt business; Anne Rose for letting us tear her house apart; William Farrington for letting us make a disgusting mess in his basement workshop; Socky for being the world's most compliant dog (when bribed with cheese); Robert Rakita for photo retouching; the author's old bachelor pals, Alan Wellikoff, Denis Boyles, and Bob Dattila for their inspiration, encouragement, and living examples of what this book should be (somebody please call the health department); and American Express, VISA, and MasterCard, whose many calls and letters provided the author with motivation to keep working.

CONTENTS

THE BACHELOR HOME COMPANION
A book about cooking, cleaning, and housekeeping for people who don't know how to do any of these things and aren't about to learn

Contents

AUTHOR'S FOREWORD
TO THE NEW EDITION

This book was written in 1986, which is half a lifetime ago in dog years and that's certainly the kind of years we're having now. When I look at these photographs of a younger (and, darn it, slimmer) self, I am suffused with nostalgia. Weren't the eighties grand? Cash grew on trees or, anyway, coca bushes. The rich roamed the land in vast herds hunted by proud, free tribes of investment brokers who lived a simple life in tune with money. Every wristwatch was a Rolex. Every car was a Mercedes-Benz. A fellow could romance a gal without shrink-wrapping his privates and negotiating the Treaty of Ghent. Communist dictators were losing their jobs, not presidents of America and General Motors. Women wore Adolfo gowns instead of dumpy federal circuit court judge robes. The Malcolm who mattered was Forbes. Bill Clinton was only a microscopic polyp in the colon of national politics, and Hillary was still in flight school, hadn't even soloed on her broom. What a blast we were having. The suburbs had just discovered Martha Stewart, the cities had just discovered crack. So many parties and none of them Democratic.

Those were halcyon (and Valium and Lithium and Prozac) days. Think of all we owe to that glorious past. And the bank. Back then health care was a tummy tuck, not an unalienable right. If you wanted a better environment, you went to Laura Ashley. Sleeping with the President meant you'd attended a Cabinet meeting. And I actually *was* a bachelor. Why didn't I listen to myself? Here is an entire treatise on the joys of the unmarried state. I not only read it, I wrote the damn book. Then I got married anyway. It's not my fault. These are the nineties, the dumb decade—dumb and complaining and sad. Fin de siècle. Fin de fun. I'm a victim, a victim of the tragic American I.Q. die-off which happened halfway through the Bush administration. I need a federal program.

There are things in this book which I wouldn't be allowed to say nowadays. The way I'm not allowed to say "gimpy," "fatso," "Mongoloid idiot" or "drunken bum." And I'm not allowed to say "ginzo," "nickel-nose," "zipper-eye," "bog trotter," "jungle bunny," "buckethead," "herring-choker," or "get a job." I'm especially not allowed to say "chick," "dame," "broad," "babe," and "okay in the hooter department." I tell you, we're going to see our sons sent home from school for writing "girl" on the bathroom wall. It's a whole new era, an era of caring and empowerment, an era devoted to concern for the disadvantaged and for the earth, which all of us share. Has anyone noticed the correlation between the hole in the ozone layer and the ever-increasing size of the bald spot on the back of Al Gore's head? In brief, it is an era characterized by some caring, empowered chick with a heinie the size of an Isuzu Trooper shrieking, *"You just don't get it!"* on national TV. Come on, honey, I'm pro-abortion, too. As long as it's retroactive.

Did I hear someone whimper "Men's Movement"? This book was never written to give blubbering pantywaists advice on achieving manhood. If you're skimming these pages in search of self-help tips, your mother dresses you funny. And you, Robert Bly, you myth-piddling dolt of posy, you are the worst versifier since the librettist for Sam the Sham and the Pharaohs. You're not fit to use No. 1 pencils on Big Chief tablets. You couldn't rhyme punt with Sinead O'Connor. (But one nice thing about having paint-covered flabby guys running around the woods with bongo drums: they're much easier to find and shoot than deer.)

A big vote of thanks to you, too, Magic Johnson. Sure, if you're getting laid eight or ten million times, you're bound to encounter "the crack of doom." For us regular guys who get lucky about once each time the planet Neptune revolves around the sun, however, Magic, you pissed in the soup. Not that we're missing much since sex became a registered trademark of the Madonna Corporation.

Welcome to these 1990s. Let us all salute (and be

sensitive to the needs of) the shiftless, the feckless, the senseless, the worthwhileness-impaired, the decency-challenged and the differently moraled. And hello to their leaders—progressive, committed and filled to the bunghole with enormous esteem for themselves. We know the type from childhood. They had their Monday's homework done by nine on Friday night. What shall their symbol be? Fasces, perhaps, though not—secular humans forbid—the old-fashioned Fascist kind. Something, nonetheless, to represent multicultural diversity's strength in the unity of P.C. thought, like, you know, whoa, "E Pluribus Unum." (Better make that bilingual.) New Age fasces—I propose a bundle of limp weenies all wound up in a "Donohue" show.

Reader, look upon this book as a relic, an antique, a souvenir of better times. Or, if you voted with your butt instead of your wallet, call it recycled. Anyway, herewith a memento of that glad epoch when we knew the proper order of words in our language—"free alcohol" not "alcohol-free"—when we preferred a shining city on a hill to a whining Hill all over Clarence Thomas, when entitlement meant being a count, when tax cuts were in bloom and Clinton was in Flowers.

I'd tell you more but suddenly I remember I was molested as a child.

— P. J. O'R.

In a backwoods cabin with four years' worth of canned good and a whole bunch of guns, 1993

PREFACE

We Are All Bachelors Now

Home life as we understand it is no more natural to us than a cage is natural to a cockatoo.
—GEORGE BERNARD SHAW

This book is addressed to the true bachelor, an adult male and a gentleman, who has never married and never intends to.

We are a select group, without personal obligation, social encumbrance, or any socks that match. We breathe the cold, pure air of solitude—of Olympus, of Parnassus, and of the basement where all the pipes are frozen because nobody turned up the thermostat. We have no need, unless puzzled by a meatloaf recipe, for dull, cloying familial ties. We are free to drop everything and mount our Rocinantes on a moment's notice.

(Although sometimes it takes a little longer than a moment because we can't remember which laundry the shirts are at.)

Sherlock Holmes was portrayed as a bachelor. So was Raffles the gentleman cracksmith. Sir Isaac Newton and Giovanni Casanova were bachelors, also St. Paul, President Buchanan, Nietzsche, Oliver Goldsmith, George "Chinese" Gordon, Voltaire, and

almost all the Popes. King Henry VIII kept trying to be one. The Lone Ranger, Sam Spade, and Jesus Christ will always be bachelors, not to mention Clarabell, Mayor Koch, and Daffy Duck.

We are our own men, aloof and independent,

We are all bachelors now, "strangers in a home we never made."

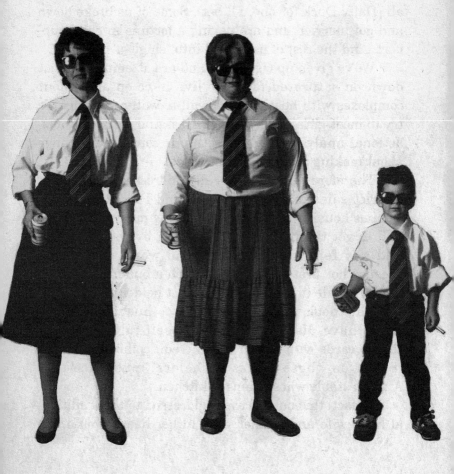

unchocked wheels in a world of cogs and gears. We do as we damn well please. And we don't belong to any immune-deficiency high-risk groups either.

We also don't exist.

What's become of the bachelors of yore? The old salts? The Oxford dons? The misanthropic billionaires wedded solely to greed? Well, some of us turned out to belong to that immune-deficiency high-risk group after all (Daffy Duck for one, I'll bet). Some of us broke down and got married and are paying a fortune in child support. And the rest of us turned into "singles."

We've given up cigarettes and are attempting to cut down on saturated fats. We live in co-op apartment complexes with heather-tone wall-to-wall carpeting. We try to meet girls at aerobics classes. And we're in transactional analysis, dealing with our conflicted feelings about making mature commitments.

Therefore this book is really addressed to assistant district sales managers, Dekes and Phi Delts in off-campus housing, divorced guys, young men who've been told to get the hell out of the house by their parents, and any fellow whose girlfriend won't marry him because her first husband was such a bummer. That is, to every male in a house without pot holders.

This book is also addressed to husbands whose wives have discovered careers, self-fulfillment, or charge cards with astronomical credit ceilings. Like the rest of us, these "grass bachelors" must face that Augean stable whose name is kitchen.

In fact, this book is even addressed to the traditional housewife and mother who, in her heart, would like to put the kids in the dog run and go play golf. Go ahead. Throw a wad of baloney in there and grab your Pings. It doesn't matter. Home life in our society has already disintegrated. Small children come home to find their parents (which, step-folks included, can number as many as ten) gone to jobs, love affairs, racketball courts, or detox centers. Old people are forced by uncaring progeny (and their own incessant complaints about what's on TV) to live in the confines of golden-age communities. Even newlyweds don't spend much time together, now that few marriages outlast the appliance warranties.

Motherly landladies and devoted kitchen help have disappeared, too—off playing seniors tennis and cheating the welfare agencies. We are all discovering anew what any ancient bond servant (or Mom, if we'd been listening) could have told us: Keeping house is as unpleasant and filthy as coal mining, and the pay's a lot worse.

So when it comes right down to it, this book is addressed to everybody. We are all bachelors now, "strangers in a home we never made."

Being a bachelor has turned me into a housewife.

INTRODUCTION

How I Became a Bachelor Housewife

If dirt was trumps, what hands you would hold!
—CHARLES LAMB

I always wanted to be a bachelor when I grew up. My friends may have had fantasies about raking the yard, seeing their loved ones in pin curlers and cleaning the garage on Sundays, but not me. I saw myself at thirty-eight lounging around a penthouse in a brocade smoking jacket. Vivaldi would be playing on the stereo. I'd sip brandy from a snifter the size of a fish tank and leaf through an address book full of R-rated phone numbers.

It never occurred to me that the penthouse would be littered with dirty socks, damp bath towels, old sports sections, and empty pizza boxes. I'd have to dig through all that stuff to find the brocade smoking jacket, and then it would need treatment with complicated spot removers. Lounging around the penthouse in an undershirt is not the same. Besides, it isn't a penthouse. Who can afford a penthouse in a job market filled with wildly competitive married guys supporting three ex-families?

I think I'll skip the brandy. You shouldn't drink on an empty stomach. I looked in the refrigerator—nothing in there except half a bottle of flat tonic water, two withered limes, and one more empty pizza box. (The brandy snifter got broken in the dishwasher anyway.)

Of course, bachelors can just go hang out in fancy restaurants all night. And I would if I weren't broke from buying new clothes. You know how it is with us fashion-conscious bachelors, always trying to keep up with the latest sartorial trends. Well, sort of. Actually, I have to buy new clothes because I destroy all my chinos and boxer shorts every time I go to the laundromat.

I used to do this with bleach and fabric softener. These made enormous piebald blotches and great big holes in my clothes. Being a suave bachelor and all, I felt it beneath my dignity to stand in a laundromat reading the instructions on the bottles. Not to mention the instructions on the machines. I might as well try to land a DC-10. What on earth is a "pre-wash cycle"? Pre-wash means "before washing." Before washing is when the clothes are scattered all over the floor. Why would I want to put money and bleach in a washing machine then? If anyone ever designs washing machines for bachelors, there will be one big dial with two settings: DIRTY and DON'T BREATHE.

Now, I just use lots of detergent. If some is good,

Washday tip: Laundromat machines are built tough. You should have no trouble doing all your laundry in one load (unless the laundromat owner catches you).

more must be better and a whole box should be great. (Another thing about washing machine instructions, they're printed on the inside of the washing machine lid. This is not where you want the instructions when the machine is spewing foam all over the laundromat and you can't even get near it, let alone open the top.) The clothes *do* get clean. True, they're stiff, have chunks of solidified laundry soap in the pockets and smell like *eau de Fab*. But that doesn't matter because I'm going to ruin them in the dryer.

The way dryers work is you put wet clothes in, run the dryer for an hour, and take wet clothes out. Leave these mildewing in a laundry bag for a couple of days, and they'll smell every bit as bad as they did before you washed them. What I recommend is insert a hundred quarters in the coin slot and go watch football games. When you come back the clothes will be dry and just the right size—if you own a doll collection. Like most bachelors, I don't.

So I got out and buy new chinos and new boxer shorts and try to save money by cooking at home. However, it's hard to make even a simple omelette with flat tonic water, withered limes, and empty pizza boxes.

The problem with grocery shopping is it lacks an element of surprise. Wait until you're very hungry before going to the store. This way you'll make lots of surprising impulse purchases. It's like Christmas when I get the grocery bags home. I don't know what might be in there—a ten-pound bag of pistachio nuts, jars of pickled squid, tinned guava jelly, goat pâté. However, it's hard to make a simple omelette with pistachio nuts, pickled squid, guava jelly, and goat pâté, too. This means another trip to the store.

Why does everything come in Giant Size, King Size, and Holy Roman Empire Size boxes? A package of macaroni as big as a Japanese car is not what I need. And I don't understand unit pricing. There's the price, the unit price, the sale price, but what does the damn thing *cost*? And I can't find stuff. Whatever I want is always thirty brands of sugar-frosted cereal away from where I am. Supermarkets should arrange it so important purchases like peanut butter, roach spray, and cigarettes are in one place, while everything else is off in a married-couple annex with the fabric softeners and breakfast foods. (Do people really feed their children purple corn flakes shaped like movie monsters? Are they mad at the kids, or what?)

I go to delicatessens because they'll bring me what I ask for. "Give me a six-pack of eggs," I say.

Bachelor cooking is a matter of attitude. If you think of it as setting fire to things and making a mess, it's fun. It's not so much fun if you think of it as dinner. Fortunately, baloney, cheeseburgers, beer, and potato-chip dip provide all the daily nutrients bachelors are known to require. I mean, I hope they do.

I have several specialties. Instant coffee is one. Simple omelettes are another. My recipe: Add contents of refrigerator to two eggs and cook until everything stops wiggling. A bachelor friend of mine has an interesting variation. Mix last night's Chinese take-out food with your scrambled eggs. (Remove fortunes from fortune cookies first.) He calls it Egg Foo Breakfast.

If you run out of clean clothes, spray deodorant can temporarily restore socks to active duty (also sport coats, blue jeans, and running shoes).

I also make a delicious stew. I put meat, beef bouillon, potatoes, celery, carrots, onions, and a splash of red wine into a large pot. When it begins to simmer I go watch football games until all the ingredients boil down to a tarry mass. Then I phone out for pizza or Chinese.

Nomenclature is an important part of bachelor

cooking. If you call it "Italian cheese toast," it's not disgusting to have warmed-over pizza for breakfast.

Pizza for breakfast is one of the great examples of bachelor freedom. And, as a bachelor, I'm free to eat pizza anywhere I want—in front of the TV or on the bed or in the bathtub. I also eat, at least to judge by where I find leftovers, in the hall closet and under the couch.

I find a lot of things under the couch whenever I clean up, giant dust bunnies mostly, but mysterious things too—rubber beach toys, copies of *Livestock Breeding Quarterly*, "Souvenir of the Seattle World's Fair" pen and pencil sets.

Maybe there are other people who live in my house and I don't know about it. I certainly don't remember putting a cigar out in the soap dish or using that new Vivaldi CD as a drink coaster or hiding my cuff links behind the thesaurus. What are my dress shoes doing in the toilet tank? Why has somebody been scaling fish on the bedroom rug?

A lot of bachelor time that married people believe is spent paging through address books is really spent using T-shirts as dust cloths and getting vacuum-cleaner cords tangled in footstools. Or thinking up reasons not to. I think, "Dirt is superficial, a matter of appearances." I think, "If you can't see dirt, it doesn't really exist." No fair looking behind the stereo speakers.

I keep the light low. Not hard when your windows need washing as badly as mine do. And forget the windows upstairs. I'd be risking my neck to wash those. What if I dropped something? A paper towel soaked in Windex might kill from that height. No use washing the dishes either. The automatic dishwasher breaks everything. I tried using paper plates, but the dishwasher made a mess of those, too.

Being a bachelor has turned me into a housewife, a lousy housewife. And now I have a different perspective on the traditional woman's role in society. A housewife has to be a chemist, engineer, mechanic, economist, philosopher, and workaholic. That's just to pick up after herself. I shudder at what it must be like when there are kids, pets, and somebody like me in the home. Therefore it is with profound respect that I ask for advice from my women friends.

"What should I do about that green fungus in the bread box?" I ask.

"I don't know," they tell me. "You'll have to talk to my husband. He does the cooking at our house. I'm pretty busy with my career."

CHAPTER 1

Basic House Cleaning

. . .we are made as the filth of the world, and are the offscouring of all things unto this day.

—I CORINTHIANS 4:13

Especially after a party.

—ANONYMOUS BACHELOR

*C*leaning, like seduction, should be done from the top down—starting with the ceiling, which is ridiculous. Gravity takes care of that. If there were any dirt on the ceiling, it would fall off and land on the floor. The same goes for the walls. Dirt falls right off them and lands on the floor. And you shouldn't fool around with the dirt on the floor because you'll stir it up and it'll get all over the walls and ceiling.

Actually, the only sensible way to clean house is to hire somebody to do it. But many of us can't afford that, and nobody will work for the rest of us. It takes special janitorial skills to cope with a bachelor household, and not many cleaning ladies are members of Hell's Angels.

How often does a house need to be cleaned, anyway? As a general rule, once every girlfriend. After that she can get to know the real you.

Don't try to kid women by being neat. Most bachelors *are* fairly neat. When the dirty clothes are stuffed in a dresser drawer, we think everything is under control, even if the floor is sticky. But women can tell tidy from clean, especially after they've leaned against a windowsill in a pair of white linen slacks.

To give a woman the impression that your house is clean, use Pledge. Don't use it *on* anything, just squirt some in the air. This makes it smell as though you've dusted. Extra-dirty areas like those windowsills can be sprayed with clear acrylic fixative, the kind artists use on charcoal sketches. This keeps dirt where it is and prevents it from rubbing off on other things. If you switch your vacuum cleaner to REVERSE, you can blow a lot of dirt out of your house. This is more enjoyable than vacuuming and you never have to empty the bag. Now spill something fresh on the floor because a slippery floor is much more like a clean, waxed floor than a sticky floor is.

Your home must be reasonably hygienic or the whole affair will have to be conducted at your girlfriend's house, and this could be a problem if she has a large husband. Also, your home shouldn't be such a disaster that you make a filthy mess of yourself trying to get to the front door to go to work. Nor should you trail the fragrance of month-old beer into the office.

But don't turn housecleaning into a job. The benefit package is lousy. And who are you going to fire when the tub looks like the Indianapolis Speedway after a nine-car pile up?

And don't be tempted to make housecleaning fun. Don't try to dust with the dog. It might *seem* like a good idea to squirt dish soap everywhere and hose the place down. After six or eight drinks it might *seem* like a hoot to get naked and slither around on the sopping wet floor with a mop head in either hand. The results will be disappointing. The house will look worse in the morning. And so will you.

And don't get too involved. There's a part of the human psyche that's never satisfied with chunks of an Archduke at Sarajevo and has to have a World War I. If you really start to *think* about cleaning house, you'll wind up on a stepladder polishing out light sockets with steel wool. Repent of thoroughness. Eschew the systematic.

Concentrate instead on preventive maintenance. Discard anything that's harder to wash than you are (Remington Model 1100 automatic shotguns and Mercedes alloy wheels excepted.) Any item of clothes or bedding that has to be dry-cleaned more often then you commit a cardinal sin in it should be thrown away. Anything that has accumulated enough dust to write your name in has to go. You aren't using it enough. It's hard to apply this advice to the woodwork but worth it.

THE KITCHEN

Every kitchen should be equipped with a dishwasher, preferably a cute one wearing her apron and nothing else. Failing this, there's the minimalist approach to avoiding dirty dishes, where you use nothing but a pair of chopsticks and your cupped hand. This is a bitch with fried eggs. Then there is the maximalist approach invented by West Coast screenwriter Bill Martin. Bill buys dishes by the box at thrift shops and Goodwill stores. When the meal is over, he puts the dishes in the sink and runs the tap until water covers them. Then he empties a dozen boxes of Jell-O into the dishwater (Bill favors lime). When the next load of dishes is dirty, the procedure is repeated with another layer of Jell-O just covering the soiled plates and glasses. Finally, when the sink is almost full, Bill puts two large pot lids into the last thickness of Jell-O. This gives him a pair of handles so he can pull the entire solidified mass out of the sink, bury it in the yard, and go buy more dishes.

Iron skillets are good because they never need washing. I mean, if you don't mind tasting what you cooked last night. And if you do mind, why did you cook it in the first place? Those black-and-white speckled graniteware pans are nice, too. They always look dirty so what's the point in cleaning them? Anyway, if you boil all your food, hot water kills germs.

Refrigerators are the only bachelor-friendly household appliances. Like anything with a lid on it, they never have to be cleaned, just sorted through occasion-

Double up on big jobs. Wait until the floor is really dirty before you wash the dishes.

ally. Refrigerated food turns directly into garbage. Unlike house dust, there are no bothersome intermediate steps. And food is good about announcing itself. Food normally comes in earth tones. When the cheese, milk, and ground beef go polychromatic, it's time for them to leave. Refrigerators also have lots of bins and trays and racks to put things in. This is as good a place as any for canned goods and rifle ammo. And refrigerators will preserve cigarettes, camera film, marijuana, and so on. I recommend having several refrigerators and putting everything in them. This way you'll never run out of cold beer and your underwear will be nice and cool in the summer.

Defrosting presents a problem, however. Especially since the freezer part of a refrigerator is necessary to make drink ice—a principal ingredient in most bachelor dinner recipes. You're never going to get the refrigerator to fit into a mircowave oven, and most microwaves won't fit into a freezer compartment. Instead, try putting the cat in the freezer and using its body heat to melt the accumulated ice. At worst, you'll be rid of the cat.

Stoves are another matter. The only thing I've ever been able to figure out about stove cleaning is to move every couple of years.

Wives and mothers use some secret method to make kitchen floors look clean. I don't mean to *get* them clean. That's easy. You wash them. But that doesn't make my floors *look* clean. It just makes them look wet. And seconds later they're covered with muddy footprints. Do housewives never let their families go outdoors? Do they put Kleenex on their shoes? Do they make the kids hang like bats from the ceiling while they make peanut-butter-and-jelly sandwiches?

The only worthwhile advice I ever got about floor cleaning was in Mexico. I was staying in a hotel in Ensenada that had a quarry tile floor. I have a quarry tile floor in my kitchen, too. Theirs looked great. Mine looks like wirephotos of a California mudslide. I asked the hotel manager how he kept the floor so shiny. ("¿Como es el floor mucho bueno . . . uh . . . kept so shiny?") "We splash a coat of diesel oil on it every day," he said.

As for the rest of the kitchen, you might as well get drunk and squirt dish soap everywhere and hose the place down after all.

THE DINING ROOM

You can keep the dining room clean by eating in the kitchen.

THE BATHROOM

And you can keep the bathroom clean by going to the bathroom in the kitchen, too, I suppose. But it doesn't sound like a good idea. You *can* cut down on bathroom mess by whizzing out the windows and using the bathtub only as a beer cooler. On the question of cleanliness you're going to have to decide between your own personal self and this room. Choose yourself. Very few women have ever come to anybody's house to kiss the sink. On the other hand, quite a few women have left because of what they found in the bathroom. It's not a good idea to let life forms breed and evolve in the sink until they've developed a civilization of their own. Maybe, every morning when you're brushing your teeth, you could just brush the sinkbowl a little bit with the toothbrush. Pretty soon you'll have a bathroom sink that looks no worse than your mouth.

In college I once tried cleaning out a toilet bowl with cherry bombs. This worked *too* well. Colored porcelain fixtures in the shade "Antique Filth" might be useful if you can find a plumber who has those in stock. Pouring paint thinner in the toilet bowl and setting it on fire melts the toilet seat.

Don't use Drano if a toilet gets clogged. Remember, the toilet is a dog's idea of Perrier. And you don't want a dog with a melted tongue. Use a wire coat hanger instead. Just drop a coat hanger in there and flush. Now you've really screwed it up. Pretty soon you catch yourself thinking, "If I'm so low on life's ladder that I have to do *this* . . . If I'm faring so poorly in my profession that I can't afford to have somebody come in even once a year in protective clothing and a mask . . . Maybe I should just give up and join the Marines."

Bathrooms can be a source of real despair. Close the door.

THE LIVING ROOM

Every month or so, take the curtains down—and throw them away. Turn the lights off if you don't want the neighbors to see what you're doing. The same goes for slipcovers. They already look worse than the chairs. Don't use any rug or upholstery shampoos. If something won't come off with hot water and Lifebuoy soap, it's probably part of the natural environment and shouldn't be tampered with. Besides, no spot remover ever made will get an old hippie pal off your couch.

Excessively clean windows are dangerous and expensive. If you can't see the glass panes, you may think the window is open and throw something through it. Confine living-room cleaning to extensive use of large plastic trash bags and vacuuming.

Use a wet/dry shop vac if you feel like a sissy with a Hoover upright. Also, the Hoover is no good for vacuuming soup. The trouble with vacuum cleaners is that you start playing with them. What will happen if I vacuum up flaming things in the ashtray? Can I catch the guppies? Will it suck all the tape out of this old Oakridge Boys 8-track cassette? How much toilet paper will come off the roll? And what will it do to the cat if he lived through defrosting the refrigerator?

In many ways a broom is just as good. You can still chase the cat with it. In the summertime I sweep everything down the living-room floor register (though I always wish I hadn't when fall comes around and the furnace goes on). In the winter I sweep everything into

Clean the ceiling? Are you crazy? Let gravity take care of that.

the fireplace, where burning it helps eliminate household odors.

A smoky fireplace does a good job of making a house smell clean—or outdoorsy, anyway. If you don't have a fireplace, leave a lit cigarette on the edge of an end table.

THE BEDROOM

Sheets can be kept clean by getting drunk and falling asleep with your clothes on. Dirty clothes can all be piled in a heap, and maybe they'll look like modern art. Or maybe they won't. The art scene is changing fast these days.

The dustballs under the bed—just let them accumulate. You may start living with a woman. And she may cheat on you. And you may come home unexpectedly. And the other man may hide under the bed. And you'll be able to find him when he sneezes because of all the dustballs. This sounds farfetched, I know. But it beats crawling around on your belly with a dustpan.

OTHER ROOMS

Close the door.

Household Cleaning Products

Many men are confused by household cleaning products. For instance, will Sani-Flush flush the dirt out of extra-filthy clothes if you put it in the washing machine? And if Comet is such a great cleanser, how come it does a lousy job on ski goggles? Below is a brief table showing the proper use of cleaning products.

Pledge—Speeds up car waxing and is satisfactory on downhill skis.

Endust—Doesn't actually "end dust," just makes everything in your house stickier than it is already. However, it will turn the cat into a carpet sweeper.

Windex—You can use Windex the way you use those little Towelettes on airplanes and give yourself an instant shower.

Spic and Span—Supposedly will clean floors without rinsing. Personally, I'm waiting for the product that will clean floors without sweeping, vacuuming, or washing.

Soft Scrub—Makes lousy toothpaste.

Toilet bowl cleaners—Use in toilet bowls, also sinks and bathtubs. They are the only thing that works on soap scum when your cleaning intervals are six months apart. (Do not use on self, pets.)

Drain cleaners—Who looks down your drains? Why clean there? Drain cleaners will, however, dissolve all organic matter, which is a good thing to know if you're planning a murder.

Ammonia—A whiff of this will clear up a stuffed nose.

Floor wax—Excellent for emergency shoeshines.

Laundry bleach—Too much eats holes in LaCoste

shirts; less won't do anything at all. Bleach is good, though, for cleaning and whitening your animal skull collection.

Saddle soap—Can be substituted for baby oil in the bedroom.

Automatic dishwasher soap—Works best if you open the box before tossing it in the automatic dishwasher.

Liquid dish soap—Great for washing the car or yourself in the shower, an excellent pet shampoo and will generally clean anything but the dishes.

Powdered laundry soap—Makes a serviceable room freshener when dumped under the couch.

Aerosol room freshener—Pressurized can is helpful for filling party balloons.

Warning

Be careful when using any of the housecleaning products listed above. Have you ever read the labels? These things contain more dangerous chemicals than Bhopal, India. Hold a lit match to the nozzle of a can of spray cleaner sometime. I'm not sure if terrorists know about this, but a flaming can of Endust can take out an armored personnel carrier, easy. These products are great for 4th of July pyrotechnics and poisoning the neighbor's Shih Tzu. But only a crazy person would leave them lying around the house. Besides costing more than an entire cleaning staff, they all stink of bogus lemon oil. Housecleaners are presumably designed to be used by women. Maybe there really is a clique of male chauvinist woman-haters running American industry, just like *Ms.* magazine says. Somebody should look into this.

TRICKING MOTHERS, LOVERS, AND FEMALE FRIENDS INTO CLEANING UP FOR YOU

Some bachelors spend years in psychoanalysis claiming to have a dependency problem with their mothers just so the old lady will come over and clean every now and then. It's hard to pull this on modern women, many of whom are in psychoanalysis themselves.

You can try being pathetically incompetent in your cleaning operation. Let your date see you wet-mopping the windows or vacuuming the dirty dishes and she may feel compelled to step in. Or she may feel compelled to step out, permanently. Knowing today's women, what your date may do is dictate a memo on proper use of housecleaning equipment and have her secretary Express Mail it to you.

Maybe you can offer to trade a woman one service for another. Tell her that if she cleans the bathroom, you'll do her taxes. By the time the IRS catches up with her, the two of you will probably have broken up.

Romance is another strategy. For some mysterious Darwinian reason, women feel compelled to straighten up bedrooms before and after sex. Try making love in every other room of the house. Suggest taking a shower together. If the woman loves you enough, she'll rush right in there with a pail and scrub brush. The only problem is, she *doesn't* love you enough. Nobody loves anybody that much. The last person to feel this strongly about someone else was Bess Truman, and she only felt that way about Harry, and they're both dead now and don't have any bathrooms to clean.

PHILOSOPHICAL, RELIGIOUS, AND HISTORICAL JUSTIFICATIONS FOR NOT CLEANING UP

Camus had it all wrong about the myth of Sisyphus. The benighted king of Corinth endlessly rolling that rock up a hill in Hell is not symbolic of life, just housekeeping. Surely there's some philosophy that will let us avoid this fate the way Existentialism lets us avoid plots in novels. But the Kierkegaards and Heideggers have spent too much time thinking about man's place in the universe and not enough time thinking about the empty TV dinner tray's place under the coffee table. Perhaps religious faith is the answer. Members of the Jainist sect in India go to extraordinary lengths to keep from taking life. The most devoted even wear veils across their mouths so they won't accidentally inhale bugs. Maybe there's some other religion that feels the same way about grease splatters on the wall above the stove. If so, I'll gladly give up being Methodist and convert.

Historically, we don't know much. No one seems to have studied ancient housekeeping. We don't know if the great civilizations of the past were slobs or what. I

This dirt cost $5.98 in a fancy plant store, but the stuff under your bed is free.

suspect that ancient Greeks were personally clean but lousy homemakers (pretty much the opposite of modern Greeks). Aristophanes doesn't strike me as the kind of guy who hung his chiton neatly on a peg when he got home from the Agora. The Romans were probably neat and clean but inclined to talk politics at the orgy. But this is just a guess. I've never been able to come up with any solid historical precedent of slovenliness that, for instance, would help me mollify a girlfriend who caught me using her electric hair curler to pluck a Canada goose.

My best arguments against housekeeping are anthropological. The definition of dirt varies greatly from one culture to another. In societies where everyone lives in huts with dirt floors, they don't consider that dirt dirt. Even in our society, women think dog hair is disgusting but silver-fox jackets that shed all over the place are cute.

But middle-class American ideas about hygiene and propriety are winning out all over the world, despite occasional rebellions. Some think of the 1960s as an era of social and political ferment. I think of them as a last doomed attempt to avoid Handi-Vacs and the steam iron. Perhaps distraction is the bachelor's only recourse. Have you noticed that when a TV is on in a room, everyone will watch the screen no matter how stupid the program? Maybe you should videotape somebody else's clean house and run the tape on your VCR. Anyway, don't make lame excuses. Try this: "You'll have to pardon the way everything looks, I'm psychotic."

CHAPTER 2

Why Have a House to Clean?

In the Big Rock Candy Mountain
You never change your socks,
And little streams of alcohol
Come a-trickling down the rocks
The boxcars all are empty
And the railroad bulls are blind,
There's a lake of stew, and whiskey, too,
You can paddle all around 'em in a big canoe
In the Big Rock Candy Mountain.

— MAC MCCLINTOCK

Why not live in hotel rooms or on tramp steamers? Why not throw some trail mix and a Sony Walkman into your frame pack and say with Wordsworth:

I wandered lonely as a cloud
That floats on high o'er vales and hills,
Then I drove to Reno for the weekend.

This thought usually strikes a bachelor when he's reading T. E. Lawrence or watching, half-drunk, a rerun of "Route 66." For a moment the idea of feckless peregrination has appeal. I'm usually halfway to the phone to call Goodwill and give my furniture away before I think again. How do I bank by mail from Samarkand? Where do I keep my beer-mug collection and my complete video library of "The World at War"? And what about health insurance or a dental plan?

The fixed abode is a recent invention, only eleven or twelve thousand years old. Still, the instinct to have one is strong. This has to do with human evolution. Other animals, when evolving, turned toenails into claws, noses into trunks, fins into thumbs, and so forth. They evolved parts of themselves. We, however, evolved parts of other animals—turning reindeer sinews into sewing thread, bearskins into bed sheets, etc. But we left ourselves alone. And we remain (except for some body hair) pretty much the way we came down from the trees. Man has experienced tremendous evolutionary progress. But our evolution is all lying around loose—we need some place to put it.

True, we can point to various primitive tribes who still haven't made permanent residence a habit. They seem happy enough. But this isn't sufficient reason for a normal civilized male to fold up his 2 x 4 studs, rafters, cement blocks, shingles, and clapboards,

Why not live in a tree?

and move them to the caribou's summer grazing range.

Man, even bachelor man, needs a home of his own. "Home," said Robert Frost, "is the place where, when you have to go there, they have to take you in." And this is especially true if nobody else lives there and the mortgage is in your name. A man's girlfriend's condo is not his castle.

A home provides privacy. You can make noise, love, a mess and not be accountable for it. In your own home you don't have to hide the pornography underneath the socks in the back of a dresser drawer. Except, of course, when the cleaning lady's due or your parents are coming over or you're going to bring a date around for a drink. So the pornography winds up in the back of the sock drawer anyway. But a home does give you a place to leave dirty laundry, which otherwise you'd have to carry around in public. And a home is a safe refuge for possessions like buffalo skulls and stuffed sailfish that no sensible person would ever let you keep in her home. Plus a home gives you something to do around the house. Furthermore, there is no real satisfaction in pissing out of somebody *else's* window.

A home gives you a mailing address so you can get credit-card bills, brochures for time-share resorts, angry letters from jilted fiancées, invitations to cousins' weddings . . . Perhaps this isn't such a strong point after all. But, if you buy your home, it's an investment. And after having the plumbers, electricians, and exterminators in, putting a new roof on, paying the taxes, and selling the place, you should be only slightly poorer than when you started.

A home keeps you from living with your parents. Albeit living with your parents, like all forms of masochism, has its comforts. At least you know where trouble's coming from and what form it will take (ditto for meals). But "lives with his mother" looks so bad in a *Who's Who* entry or on campaign literature if you happen to be running for political office. Also it puts a crimp in your romantic life.

And a home of your own has emotional benefits. Modern psychiatry has shown that the desire to return to the womb is a normal, even healthy part of our natural makeup. How much more so if that womb has cable TV and a liquor cabinet.

WHAT KIND OF HOME TO HAVE

Not a boat. Never buy anything that already leaks. This is a good general principle in life and can be applied to human shelter, cantaloupes, flashlight batteries, jars of spaghetti sauce, used cars, babies, and most other stuff. In particular, don't buy anything that leaks from the wrong end. Homes are supposed to leak from the top end. This is not a problem. You can put a bucket under the leak when it rains. But boats leak from the bottom end and note what happens when you put a bucket under the leak in a boat. First, you lose the bucket. And because you had to go underwater to do this, the bucket was full anyway. Also consider going to bed drunk. The

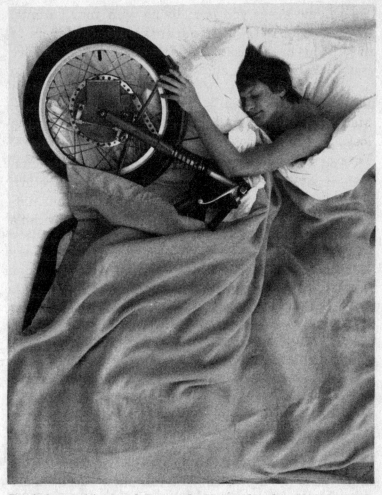

Don't forget, it's your home and you can do what you want.

bed—that is, the berth—is spinning as usual, but it's also rolling and pitching and heaving and yawing and... Ooooooo, quick, where's the bathroom, I mean head?

WACK! Ouch! The next thing you know you've cracked your skull on the spar or the boom or the mast or the yard or one of those damn things that's always in your way when you have to throw up on a boat.

Even so, bachelors are often tempted to make their homes afloat, especially bachelors who read John D. MacDonald books, and all of us do. Living on a boat looks so good in Scotch ads and women find boats sexy. Wrong. Women find boats sexy until they discover they have to go to the toilet with their knees under the sink and there's no tub or blow dryer.

What women actually find sexy is a real house, the two-story kind with trees in the yard. This stimulates the nest-making gland, turning women warm, cozy, and wholesomely lubricious. Now's your chance. Kiss them quick. Get them rolling between the bed sheets in the first half-hour. And I don't give this advice from any satyr-like motive. It's just that, if you don't catch that first surge of glandular sexuality, the hormones continue to accumulate and change into something quite different, and instead of romance you'll get Laura Ashley wallpaper in the dining room and guest towels that match the bathmat.

There are other advantages to having a real house. It gives you something to put the garage behind. And you can burn a house or blow it up, which is generally illegal with an apartment building. And there's a psychological wholeness to a house. Symbolically, there's a basement for the dark, primordial drives of the id, a first floor where the ego resides, and an upstairs for the superego with its work ethic (this is why the typewriter always goes in the spare bedroom) and its bad con-science about what you did with that young lady who came over to see the place. A real house has a personali-ty, a voice of its own.

"Food! Sex! Nap time!" says the id in the basement.

"Look at this Bokhara rug. That sucker cost two thousand bucks," says the ego in the living room.

"Will you two shut up!" yells the superego in the spare bedroom. "I'm trying to write!"

Actually, this doesn't sound like psychological wholeness. This sounds like schizophrenia. Maybe an apartment is better after all.

In an apartment the basement belongs to somebody else, thank God. The id has to go sack and pillage in the outdoors, which also belongs to somebody else. So do the other sides of the walls and this gives you only half as much to worry about wall-wise. And when something in the apartment doesn't work, there's a landlord or a super to call. He won't fix it, of course, but if this were your house and there were no landlord you wouldn't fix it either.

Thus an apartment is probably the bachelor home of choice. Although a house is the sexiest and therefore preferable. And a boat is the easiest to clean because you can turn it upside down and wash it out, usually by accident.

Don't even think about "alternative" homes such as tents, yurts, geodesic domes, and underground solar sod houses. These are always stuck off in the woods somewhere. Woods are full of squirrels, bears, rac-coons, etc. Yet you never see any of those animals constructing geodesic domes. Animals are no fools—they commute.

Anyway, tents are more cramped than New York City studio apartments and leakier than sailboats and are going to smell worse than either pretty soon, because it's a long way to the shower. No woman is going to sleep with you in a tent if she can possibly help it. Plus there's always a hole in the air mattress and a pinecone under her behind and the fire's gone out and she thinks she hears snakes and . . . forget it.

And forget trailer parks. Trailer parks attract brief, trashy newspaper items and irate husbands with guns. Read some brief, trashy newspaper items about irate husbands with guns and you'll see—when they shoot bachelors, it's usually in a trailer park.

WHERE TO HAVE YOUR HOME

A rural home is almost as bad as a tent in the woods. True, you have complete privacy and can turn up the stereo as loud as you want and have orgies for days on end. The problem is there's no one to have those orgies with and the nearest decent record store is fifty miles away. You're going to wind up romping around naked with the golden retriever and listening to your old Jay and the Americans albums for the rest of your life.

A city is better, except for all these sexually transmitted contagions hitting the headlines every time you take off your pants. There are also too many steady jobs in the city, and you may be tempted to take one. A steady job is at least as deleterious to the spirit of bachelorhood as a steady date. Some jobs are worse than actual wives. Ad agency *vs.* matrimony, for instance: Even the most capricious and demanding spouse is not going to divorce you for refusing to spend forty hours a week making up lies about toilet paper.

Suburbs are the best. Suburbs used to be staid and filled with prying neighbors. But that was before divorce, drugs, and Alzheimer's disease. Larchmont, Lake Forest, and Shaker Heights are now filled with lonely wives and unsupervised daughters. Practically everybody has a Jacuzzi in the rec room. And because suburban police departments are notably second-rate, a lot of other things are going on, too. Suburbs have all the sins and most of the conveniences of big cities plus you can find a parking place and the muggers are only semi-pro.

In sum, the conclusion about a home for the single male is that the ideal bachelor pad is a house in the suburbs. This sounds depressing. This is depressing. Life is depressing. And bachelorhood, like being alive, is more depressing than anything but the known alternative.

Bachelor Safety Tip

Never throw food on a grease fire.

42

WHAT TO DO WITH YOUR HOME
NOW THAT YOU HAVE ONE

A married man's home gives him something to come back to. But a bachelor's home does better than that—it gives him something to leave. And considering what a mess it is, the sooner the better.

CHAPTER 3

Bachelor Cooking, Part One

Alas! What various tastes in food,
Divide the human brotherhood!
Birds in their little nests agree
With Chinamen, but not with me.
The French are fond of slugs and frogs,
The Siamese eat puppy-dogs.
In Italy the traveler notes
With great disgust the flesh of goats
Appearing on the table d'hôtes;
And even this the natives spoil
By frying it in rancid oil.

—HILAIRE BELLOC

There's only one secret to bachelor cooking—not caring how it tastes. If you achieve this, everything will be fine. Being a bachelor is, in this sole respect, like being a Buddhist mendicant. Wandering monks are expected to eat, without pleasure or distaste, whatever is put in their begging bowls. That shows they have transcended desire. There's a story about one monk who had a leper's finger fall in his bowl. The monk ate it and promptly attained enlightenment. And this is the enlightenment he attained: "TV dinners aren't so bad if you remember to peel the foil back from the custard thingy."

That's all there is to know. The rest is damage control—most of which can be done with Tabasco sauce or common antacids.

There's no denying, however, that bachelor cooking is dangerous. Poisoning and starvation are two hazards. But they are nothing compared to the horror of creeping gourmetism. Do *not* get interested in food preparation. The world doesn't need another Felix Unger. The spectacle of a grown man discussing basil leaves is repulsive to all sensitive people. Your friends would rather die and a hundred times rather go to a restaurant than sit around in your fool kitchen watching you put water chestnuts where they don't belong and make a disgusting mess with romaine lettuce.

What would have happened if Paleolithic man had stayed in the cave all day, lightly braising mammoth chops? The women would have had to hunt mammoth, and you know how women are. Instead of just driving the thing over a cliff, they would have enticed their mammoth into a primitive barn stall, fed it leftovers, washed and curried it, and tied rawhide ribbons in its fur. Then, the next time you wanted to lightly braise some mammoth chops, the women would scream, "Kill Muffin?! How could you!" and start to cry.

Besides, if you were a cook, you'd know it already. You'd have one of those hats.

Cooking is a complicated business. You don't just start in on it overnight because you're tired of Underwood deviled ham. You're probably tired of going to the dentist, too, but that doesn't mean you're going to take a Black and Decker and a can of spackle and have a go at your molars while looking in the bathroom mirror.

And remember these two important points:

1.What you cook isn't going to be any good anyway.
2.I'm not kidding.

BASIC KITCHEN EQUIPMENT

The bachelor cook needs a fully equipped kitchen. Like a hole in the head. Keep these items on hand:

- Buck knife
- Fire extinguisher
- Bottle of Jack Daniel's
- Long stick
- Aspirin
- Alka-Seltzer
- Hungry dog to eat what you've ruined

No need to bother with complicated popcorn poppers. Just toss five pounds of popcorn kernels into the oven with a stick of margarine and set to 450°.

Whisks, ladles, slotted spoons, cheese graters, garlic presses, vegetable peelers, potato mashers, and all the rest of that stuff is good for nothing but falling out of the cup rack and jamming the rotor in the bottom of the automatic dishwasher.

Blenders are good for making the kind of drinks that women don't think are drinks and drink too much of. Then they get sick, instead of cuddly. You can also put leftover manicotti in the blender with a tray of ice cubes and some milk and call it "frozen frappé à la Romano."

Microwave ovens, too, are best used as toys. Crumple up aluminum foil and watch it spark in there. See what microwaves do to a sealed can of creamed corn. Find out if the thing will dry slush-soaked dress shoes. (So much for the $200 Bally tassel loafers.) But for actual cooking you'll find food that comes out of a microwave is every bit as bad as food that comes out of a regular oven, just quicker. Therefore you're not as hungry. So the food tastes even worse than it was going to, and that was bad enough. Also, microwaves don't give you time to have five or six flavor-deadening drinks while the Swanson Hungry-Man Salisbury Steak Dinner is getting black around the edges.

Cuisinarts can do absolutely nothing that a restaurant can't do better. And since a fully tricked-out Cuisinart costs about as much as a restaurant, buy a steakhouse instead.

Toasters are all right. But toast gets cold so fast. And you can make your own cold toast by leaving bread slices out on the counter top until they get rock hard (color with cinnamon). Don't cook steaks in the toaster, even little ones. I've tried this and the fire department comes.

COOKING TECHNIQUES

Boiling

Practically anything can be boiled. Then again, practically anything can be eaten. If you have to. Boiling works best on instant coffee, pasta, potatoes, ocean animals that are still alive, and things you aren't going to eat anyway, like vegetables. Boiling kills the mouth-full-of-garden-mulch taste most vegetables have and also destroys boring vitamins so you don't have to feel guilty about leaving your vegetables untouched.

Hint: Things boil fastest when you're on the phone.

Poaching

This is a fancy word for boiling. When somebody suggests, "Let's have poached fish," say to yourself, "Let's have boiled fish," and talk them out of it. Poached eggs are a sort of Polish joke about hardboiling: You break the eggs when they're raw and *then* boil them. What you get is egg soup.

Simmering

Trying to boil something in a pot so huge the water never comes to a boil and you have to go out at midnight and look for a restaurant that's open.

Steaming

Cooking things in the sauna, which is about all the sauna's good for now that diseases have made promiscuity unfashionable.

Baking

What you'd call using the oven if you knew how to use the oven.

Roasting

Baking that makes an extra-large mess.

Broiling

Ruining a piece of meat one side at a time instead of all at once. Broiling lets you cook a steak that, when mathematically averaged, is medium rare.

All real bachelor food is fried. Melt some butter in an iron skillet and you practically can't go wrong.

Flambéing

This generally happens by accident. To your dinner guests you say "flambé"; to the insurance agent you say, "short in the house wiring."

Sautéing

Done for health reasons. If you put oil in a skillet and fry something, women and married friends holler about cholesterol and cardiac arrest. But if you put oil in a skillet and sauté something, it's all right.

Frying

All real bachelor food is fried, preferably in butter or bacon fat or lard and never in chrysanthemum oil or mung-sprout shortening or any other kind of fake grease that tries to pass itself off as good for you. Grease is the key ingredient in bachelor cooking. Grease makes food taste greasy, which is better than having it taste like a bachelor cooked it. And if you roll the greasy food around in flour before you cook it, you've got three of the four Unmarried-Male Food Groups: fat, grease, starch, and sugar. (You can get the sugar, too, if you have a Mai Tai with dinner.)

If you fry vegetables in enough butter, you can turn even squash into real food, the kind that absorbs excess booze and keeps the circulatory system busy all month.

Most canned foods like hash, baked beans, and Beefaroni should be fried. Fry eggs (of course), bread (if you want to), soup (sort of), and oatmeal, cookie dough, and fruit cocktails (why not?). Fried cottage cheese is probably okay, although I haven't personally tried it. A fried peanut butter sandwich is surprisingly good.

You just can't go wrong with a hot skillet and a pound of Bossy's best. Plus you can cut out the little picture of a butter box on the Land O' Lakes label and fold the package so that the Indian girl's knees show through the hole and it looks like she's got her blouse open.

INGREDIENTS

Meat

This vital bachelor nutrient is commonly found in grease, therefore your daily minimum meat intake is more or less guaranteed.

Despite the fact that meat is made from dead animals, it shouldn't smell that way. Try this test for meat freshness: close your eyes and see if you can tell the pork chops from a gym locker.

Almost all varieties of meat are good enough to be better then vegetables, except veal. Veal is a very young beef and, like a very young girlfriend, it's cute but boring and expensive. Veal will eventually grow into something worthwhile like a steak, but it won't do this in your refrigerator. Also veal is too well-liked by the kind of people who think all food is better for you if it tastes like the bag it came in.

There are many different cuts of meat, all of which are fine, but remember that anything more than eight inches thick is going to fry slowly and be hard to flip with a spatula. The U.S. government grades meat and the system they use is as comprehensible as most things the government does. Just stay away from U.S.D.A. School Lunch Grade.

Poultry

Poultry is like meat, except when you cook it rare. Then it's like bird-flavored Jell-O.

Fish

You have to wonder about a food that everybody agrees is great except that sometimes it tastes like what it is.

Shellfish

Never serve oysters during a month that has no paycheck in it.

Eggs

Good: chicken eggs, goose eggs, duck eggs, plover eggs, quail eggs, sturgeon eggs, shad eggs

Pretty good: ostrich eggs, turtle eggs, Egg McMuffins

Terrible: powdered eggs, L'Eggs

Soup

What to call stew or spaghetti sauce that just didn't come together.

Salads and greens

Mopsy! Flopsy! Cottontail! Dinner is served! . . . I mean, would you go out and graze in the yard?

Salad is so seventies, like platform shoes and disco. Still, if you feel you must have salad, a can of Pam aerosol cooking oil makes salad-tossing easy, even fun. Stay away from the goofier kinds of lettuce. Any lettuce that comes from the store in a form that can't be thrown from third base to home is too exotic.

Vegetables

Never trust a man who raves about fresh-cooked vegetables. (See "Frying," above.) There *are* a few vegetables that are better than not eating at all—the first asparagus of the season, sweet corn stolen out of a field and cooked over an open fire when you're twelve. But most vegetables are something God invented to let women get even with their children.

The only really good vegetable is Tabasco sauce. Put Tabasco sauce in everything. Tabasco sauce is to bachelor cooking what forgiveness is to sin. The next best vegetable is the jalapeño pepper. It has the virtue of turning salads into practical jokes.

Fruit

A fruit is a vegetable with looks and money. Plus, if you let fruit rot, it turns into wine, something Brussels sprouts never do.

Grease

See the section on Frying in "Cooking Techniques" for a more complete discussion of this marvelous sub-

---

Bachelor Health Tip

Remember, your body needs 6 to 8 glasses of fluid daily. Straight up or on the rocks.

---

stance. It gets better with age. I've found Bacon Drippings '84 is particularly good. Keep grease in a convenient container near the stove—the dirty skillet that it's in already, for instance.

Cereals and grains

Remember the scene in *Taxi Driver*, when Robert De Niro pours Scotch on his corn flakes? That's what happens to bachelors who fool with breakfast cereals. They go crazy. Bran in particular is a sign of mental aberration. And a bachelor who eats wheat germ probably also gets Radio Moscow on his bridgework. Coffee and cigarettes are much better if you want an instant breakfast.

Pastas

They're great. But there must be some way to turn them into finger food. Try the microwave.

Bread

Commercial white bread, though not food by any stretch of the imagination, does turn anything you put between two slices of it into lunch. No home should be without some.

Bachelor Cooking, Part One

Cookies, pies, cakes, candies, and ice cream

A good bachelor drinks his dessert (and sometimes the rest of his meals). A sweet tooth is a danger signal that you're getting too much exercise and not enough cocktails.

Canned goods and frozen foods

Precooked foods require faith. If you doubt that Franco-American spaghetti is spaghetti, you'll be unhappy. But if you believe it's extra-thick tomato soup with noodles, you'll be okay.

Frozen dinners can be cooked very effectively in the fireplace—or just thrown in there. They burn longer and smell better than a Duraflame log.

Condensed soups are best if you don't put water in them, just leave them condensed. Or, better yet, leave them in the can.

Combine various canned goods and you may create a masterpiece—or an excuse to visit Burger King. Sloppy Joe mix is very good for this. Try Sloppy Peas, Sloppy Hash, Sloppy Fried Rice. Tuna is another excellent bulking agent. Try combining Campbell's condensed cream of mushroom with tuna for a soup/stew/sandwich spread. Or start with pork and beans in a large pot and add any other canned goods you've got. When you've forgotten what's in there, it's ready.

Spices and flavorings

Salt keeps your blood pressure up to the pitch of modern life and improves all foods. Without salt, pretzels would be nothing but breadsticks with bad posture and potato chips would be potatoes. Use salt in everything.

(Incidentally, it's the salt in an olive that gives a martini its snap. You can use a tiny pinch of table salt to make an emergency martini when you're out of olives and cocktail onions. Be careful, though. If you add too much salt, you'll wind up with a Margaritatini, which is awful.)

Pepper. Use everywhere you use salt, except the icy driveway.

Ketchup, the all-purpose flavor end-run. Should be used on anything that would be inedible if it didn't have ketchup on it.

Mustard is useful for cutting the excessively ketchupy taste so many foods have.

Sugar. Use anywhere salt doesn't seem to do the trick, e.g., in coffee and Kool-Aid, or on shredded wheat.

Lemon juice, an important ingredient in Bloody Marys and other forms of liquid breakfast. Makes fish taste as if it was grown on trees. And improves, immensely, the taste of lemons.

Wine splashes are vital when cooking for your date. A splash of wine turns anything into haute cuisine, at least early in a relationship. It looks as though you're making an effort. Of course, if you really were, you'd take her out to Lutèce. But a bottle of Gallo Hearty

Burgundy is a lot cheaper and usually closer to the bedroom.

Worcestershire sauce, a boon for spoilage control. Makes meat that's a bit off taste like meat that's a bit off in an expensive restaurant.

Sage, rosemary, and thyme make lamb taste like Simon and Garfunkel records.

Oregano makes everything taste like pizza.

Saffron makes everything taste bright yellow.

Tarragon. Put it in vinegar if you want to impress salad eaters.

Parsley, the only condiment you look at rather than eat. Who knows why? But when the parsley and the meat get to be the same color, throw the meat away.

Garlic keeps vampires—and everybody else—away.

Marijuana makes everything, including the dog's dinner, taste absolutely delicious. As a result, this spice should never be used by bachelors whose age or waistline exceeds thirty-five.

Bay leaves. It's much more polite for guests to choke on one of these than on your cooking. If you don't have a bay leaf handy, an oak or elm leaf will do.

Regular. One of my favorite flavors, as in "Regular Crest." I don't know exactly what's in it, but I'll bet it could make lots of things taste better than they do when I cook them.

Tobacco. No matter how long you've been a bachelor and no matter how much you've had to drink, you can't put tobacco in food.

Hamburger Helper. It doesn't help.

General note on the use of seasoning: Use enough so

Bachelor Diet Tip

Eating doesn't make you fat. Marriage does. Compare waistlines of married and single friends for proof. But yogurt *does* make good shaving cream.

---

you're not just wasting time standing around with a bottle of ground plant leaves in your hand. But don't use so much that people in the next block can smell it with their windows closed.

CHAPTER 4

Bachelor Cooking,
Part Two

"Recipe—A series of step-by-step instructions for preparing ingredients you forgot to buy in utensils you don't own to make a dish the dog won't eat the rest of."

—HENRY BEARD AND ROY McKIE,
A Cook's Dictionary

$\mathcal{M}$any cookbooks claim their recipes are simple. But follow the instructions and the next thing you know you're up to your nose in larding needles and double boilers, trying to make béarnaise sauce with chip dip and milk out of the cat's bowl. The following recipes, however, really are simple, having met these four stern bachelor criteria:

1. Quick

2. Require ingredients you probably have already and that are definitely available at the 7-11

3. Involve foodstuffs able to withstand overcooking, undercooking, house fires, and being dropped on the floor

4. Have instructions so simple you don't have to follow them

These recipes also produce lousy results. But you can't have everything.

THE SEVEN ESSENTIAL BACHELOR MEALS

Standard-issue breakfast

Orange juice, coffee, scrambled eggs, toast, and bacon—it's a meal suitable for any time of day, even morning.

You can squeeze your own orange juice by putting oranges in a big plastic garbage bag and stepping on them. Or just buy it. Fresh coffee can be brewed by tying up the grounds in a clean white athletic sock and boiling. This is only a little worse than instant coffee. If you've lost your toaster or are using it to dry your duck-hunting hat, lay bread or muffin slices right on the stove burners. Bacon is hard to wreck if you put it in the oven (use a pan or the lid off something), and set the heat for 350° or 400°. Throw some frozen Tater Tots in with the bacon—delicious, and it lets you perform messy grease cleanup with your own stomach.

The secret to scrambled eggs is a big two-fingered scoop of butter for each egg, and low heat so they don't catch fire and make the house smell like burning dog hair. You'll be tempted to add various things to the scrambled eggs, and you're going to give in to this temptation. Just follow this simple rule: Never put an ingredient into scrambled eggs that would make you gag if it weren't in scrambled eggs, i.e., turkey livers.

An interesting variation on the standard-issue breakfast is Floaters, or Death Over Easy. Tear up half a pound of bacon strips with your hands, throw them into a skillet and make grease. Break a couple of eggs into the pan and slop the hot grease over the eggs until they're done. Serve with Bufferin and a bullshot (vodka in beef bouillon).

Real hamburgers

The secret to getting that compelling/disgusting burger flavor that only roadside bars and all-night diners seem able to achieve is:

1. Cheap ground beef that's at least 30% fat and 20% filler
2. A dirty skillet (readily available in most bachelor households)

Moosh the burger patty down flat, put a bookend or

doorstop on top of it, and turn the stove flame up high so that everything gets splattered. Use heaps of salt and pepper and only the gooiest untoasted burger buns. Garnish according to how wide you can open your mouth.

To make a cheeseburger, be sure to use cheese *food*, not real cheese. Atomic breeder reactors cannot melt real cheese. Slip the cheese slice on top of the meat after the initial doorstop squashing, and cover skillet with something (not your hand) until cheese food drips onto skillet surface and looks like coal tar. Serve with beer, chips, another hamburger, more beer.

Peanut-butter-and-jelly sandwich classic

Proportion is everything. There has to be just enough jelly to squirt out between the bread slices and just enough peanut butter to keep it from doing so. Use the freshest commercial white bread. Wonderbread is okay but Sunbeam and Silvercup are better. Cheap jelly is also essential. Welch's Grapelade is the best. And use a brand of peanut butter that has at least a $5 million annual TV ad budget. Skippy, Jif, and Peter Pan are recommended. Health-food-store peanut butter is good only for cabinet-making repairs. Homemade jams, gourmet jellies, marmalade, etc., are unthinkable. And never use French bread, wheat bread, rye bread, pumpernickel, croissants, or English muffins, though hot-dog buns will do in a pinch. It's also acceptable to use saltines.

Appendix No. 1: Bachelor Measuring

TABLE OF EQUIVALENTS

Bachelor Measuring Units		Customary Household Measuring Units
1 shotglass	=	3 tablespoons
1 handful (dry measure)	=	1/3 cup
1 cupped hand (liquid measure)	=	1/2 cup
1 mouthful	=	1/3 cup
1 good splash (from tap)	=	4 tablespoons
1 good splash (from wine bottle)	=	1/2 cup
1 good splash (from whiskey bottle into highball glass)	=	6 fluid ounces
1 beer can	=	1 cup
1 dog dish	=	1 pint

TABLE OF EQUIVALENTS

Customary Household Measuring Units		Bachelor Measuring Units
1 teaspoon	=	too much salt
1 tablespoon	=	too much instant coffee
1 cup	=	too much mixer
1 pint	=	not enough whiskey
1 quart	=	too much gin
1 gallon	=	enough beer to last until half-time
1 peck	=	I forgot to buy sweet corn
1 bushel	=	I bought too much
1 pound	=	3 oz. of T-bone steak after 15 minutes on the grill

Mouse in Aspic—an example of overambitious bachelor cooking.

Grilled cheese sandwich
à la home from school for lunch

Let me again emphasize the importance of cheese food, where Velveeta reigns supreme. Any attempt to use Brie, Camembert, Gouda, or even presliced Swiss will get you drummed out of the International Brotherhood of Bachelors, and you'll have to go teach ballroom dancing. Commercial white bread is also important here, but in this case it can be as stale as a hockey puck.

Melt too much butter in a skillet and thoroughly slop all sides of the bread. Set at medium heat and crush sandwich with a dinner plate. This will reduce the finished product to an authentic one-eighth-inch thickness, while greasing the bottom of your plate so it won't stick to the kitchen table.

Serve with chocolate milk and Campbell's chicken noodle soup for an afternoon of total regression.

Steak

Every bachelor believes that there's one dish he knows how to cook. For 98 percent of us this is steak. And we're right. Even we can cook a steak, especially if we don't get silly with the broiler or the charcoal grill and just fry it in a pan.

Buy the most expensive steak you can find, about as thick as the heel of a Bass Weegun. Salt and pepper it liberally and don't worry that salting the steak before

Appendix No. 2: Spoilage Table

How to Tell When Foodstuffs Should Be Discarded

The Gag Test Anything that makes you gag is spoiled except for leftovers from what you cooked for yourself last night.

Eggs When something starts pecking its way out of the shell, the egg is probably past its prime.

Dairy Products Milk is spoiled when it starts to look like yogurt. Yogurt is spoiled when it starts to look like cottage cheese. Cottage cheese is spoiled when it starts to look like regular cheese. Regular cheese is nothing but spoiled milk anyway and can't get any more spoiled.

Mayonnaise If it makes you violently ill after you eat it, mayonnaise is spoiled.

Frozen Foods Frozen foods that have become an integral part of the defrosting problem in your freezer compartment will probably be spoiled—or wrecked, anyway, by the time you pry them out with a kitchen knife.

Meat If opening the refrigerator door causes stray animals from a three-block radius to congregate outside your house, the meat is spoiled.

Lettuce Bibb lettuce is spoiled when you can't get it off the bottom of the vegetable crisper without Comet.

Canned Goods Any canned goods that have become the size or shape of a basketball should be disposed of. Carefully.

Carrots A carrot that you can tie a clove hitch in is not fresh.

Wine It should not taste like salad dressing.

Potatoes Fresh potatoes do not have roots, branches, or dense, leafy undergrowth.

Chip Dip If you can take it out of its container and bounce it on the floor, it has gone off.

N.B.: Most food cannot be kept longer than the average life-span of a hamster. Keep a hamster in your refrigerator to gauge this.

Modern electrical appliances help take the work out of serving large meals.

it's cooked will make it tough. Salt does not make steaks tough. Poverty makes steaks tough, sometimes absent entirely. Put half a shot glass of any kind of oil but motor or olive in a skillet. Heat it up until the oil smokes like hell. Now take the batteries out of your smoke detector and put the steak in the pan. Fiddle with the steak, turn it over a lot and poke it constantly with a fork and knife. This does nothing for the steak, but it keeps you from wandering off and starting to watch a basketball game and turning the T-bone into a flight jacket. As soon as you think the steak should cook just a little longer, stop cooking it.

Serve with whiskey and warmed-over french fries from McDonald's.

Spaghetti Divorce Style

Boil spaghetti until it sticks to the wall when you throw it across the room. Drain through window screen or ex-girlfriend's fishnet stockings or the like. While this is going on, heat up a jar of Ragu spaghetti sauce and put things into it. As with scrambled eggs, the hard part here is stopping yourself once you've begun adding ingredients. Spaghetti is rarely fixed sober, and it may seem like a good idea to put everything in the house into the spaghetti sauce. This is not true.

ROUGH GUIDE TO SPAGHETTI SAUCE INGREDIENTS: WHAT SHOULD AND SHOULD NOT BE ADDED

Yes	Maybe	No
spaghetti	egg noodles	beans
oregano	fresh basil	celery
garlic salt	garlic cloves	candy and gum
ground beef	baloney	dessert topping
tomato paste	steamed tomatoes	stewed fruit
chopped onions	cocktail onions	Brussels sprouts
pepperoni	breakfast sausage	head cheese
leftover steak tips	leftover veal piccata	leftover burritos
wine	beer	whiskey
anchovies	sardines	tuna
hot peppers	sugar	mayonnaise
	Bac-O-Bits	raisin bran
	smoked clams	bananas
		flan
		baking soda
		yams
		lettuce

Genuine Texas Six-Gun Double-Toilet Chili

The recipe is exactly the same as the recipe for spaghetti sauce, except take out the spaghetti and add everything in the "No" column above.

THREE CULINARY EXPERIMENTS FOR THE ADVENTUROUS

Doggy Melt

Boil or heat a hot dog or leave it out to get warm. Put it on a piece of toast or bread with a slice of Velveeta cheese on top and put the whole thing in the oven. Doggy melts make a great plea for help. Fix these to make women feel sorry for you.

Girlfriend Chicken

Put a raw chicken breast into a pot with a lid and pour the contents of a can of condensed cream of mushroom soup in there. Put the pot in the oven and cook at 350° until you can bite into the chicken without gagging. You can pour the results over a big pile of toast if you want to.

This dish is customarily fixed by girl bachelors—your girlfriend, for instance. But you may not have a girlfriend, and if you live according to the precepts of this book, you may not get one. So you can fix it for yourself. Seasoning may help. Or it may not. You might be able to put a potato in the mushroom soup. Maybe you should even boil it first. I have no idea.

Appendix No. 3: Emergency Helps

Cooking Without Utensils

- Cook a toasted cheese sandwich by wrapping sandwich in aluminum foil and ironing it with a steam iron. A steam iron can also be turned upside-down and held in place with books to make a hot plate.
- Fix breakfast by balancing unbroken raw eggs between the pipes of a steam radiator before you go to bed.
- Make your own beef jerky by letting meat sit out on the countertop for a week.
- Dangle a cube steak in front of a blow dryer.
- Warm canned goods by putting them inside the air-cleaner on your car engine and driving around at 100 miles an hour.
- Bacon can be made to cook itself if you light it with a Zippo.
- Turn TV dinners directly into cold leftovers by allowing them to thaw.
- Use a low-speed electric drill to turn any fire into a rotisserie.
- Take a hint from beef tartare and use your imagination to turn raw hamburger into food.
- Five main courses that can be fixed with only a Buck knife:
    1. cold peas on Melba toast
    2. pasta shavings in milk
    3. minced baloney in pineapple halves
    4. hearts of canned ham
    5. salami carved into the shape of a submarine

Tuna Whatsit

This is really horrible. The only reason you'd fix this is to show your ex-wife or your parole officer that you're trying to live like a human.

Mix a whole bunch of canned tuna with the now familiar condensed mushroom soup and a can of peas. It should achieve the consistency of Play-Dough. Put the result into something that won't explode in the oven—empty Chinese-food containers work well—and crumble potato chips over the top. Cook for as long as it takes to watch a ball game on TV.

MENU PLANNING

Below is a complete week of menus designed to meet the need of single men. These meals will provide a balanced, well-rounded diet for the typical bachelor if combined with cigarettes and whiskey.

Monday

Breakfast: Twinkies
Lunch: Beef jerky sandwich
Dinner: Hot fudge Mrs. Paul's Frozen Fish Sticks sundae

Bachelor Cooking, Part Two

Tuesday

Breakfast: Potato-chip dip eaten with a spoon
Lunch: Dinty Moore beef stew, lettuce, and tomato sandwich
Dinner: Noodles and booze

Wednesday

Breakfast: Special K in mouthwash
Lunch: Bac-O-Bits sandwich
Dinner: Pizza Cheetos

Thursday

Breakfast: Powdered soup in tap water
Lunch: Shake and Bake sandwich
Dinner: Maraschino cherry omelette

Friday

Breakfast: Cashews and Cool Whip
Lunch: Tabasco and mayonnaise sandwich
Dinner: Aerosol cheese spread and anchovy paste on brown-and-serve rolls

Saturday

Breakfast: Aspirin and warm beer
Lunch: Lipton iced tea mix sprinkled over warm toast
Dinner: Minute Rice à la mode

Sunday

Brunch: Vodka and Hi-C
Dinner: Cookies and water

ADVANCED BACHELOR COOKING

Advanced bachelor cooking is done only for the benefit of others, though "benefit" may not be the right word. Anyway, it's only done when other people are around. Let's hope they're easygoing people. Let's also hope they had the sense to eat before they left home.

Charcoal cooking

All bachelors—in fact, all men—think they know how to cook over charcoal, even if otherwise they can't get cellophane off lettuce. Two rules should be remembered: Always do it outdoors, or at least on the porch,

Put a stick through the middle of anything to give it that out-doorsy flavor.

Horrible Bachelor Refrigerators

There's nothing worse than this kind of bachelor refrigerator . . .

except this kind of bachelor refrigerator.

never in the sink. And don't charcoal-grill anything you don't want ruined. It's horrible to see good steaks turned into meat ash. It's even sad to see hot dogs napalmed. Instead, cook up some slabs of semi-edible sport fish, like tarpon or hammerhead shark. Incineration always improves fish. Stouffer's frozen entrées are another perfect choice. Better yet, forget the charcoal fire and just put a stick through the middle of anything to give it that outdoors flavor. Try this with a ham.

But it's no use. Nothing can keep men from attempted arson when it comes to food. I hesitate to even mention luau pits and clambakes. Consider the absurdity of these cooking methods. Just try doing anything with a hot rock. Try ironing a shirt. What makes you think roasting a pig with it is going to be any easier? Anyway, be a good camper and make sure the fire is out when you're done. (In my personal experience the best way to do this is by putting food in it.)

Game cooking

The other kind of cooking men think they know how to do is game cooking. Though the idea of eating our little forest pals is so repulsive to most guests that no one ever finds out what the meal tastes like. What it tastes like, by the way, is militant liver.

Wild game does have one thing in common with food: It kills the appetite, and that's what eating is all about. The following recipe for duck is as good a way to

Appendix No.4: Emergency Helps

Cooking Without Food

Emergency Tomato Soup
Made with hot water and ketchup. (Cold water and ketchup makes Emergency Bloody Mary Mix.)

Emergency PB&J Sandwich
There's always *some* peanut butter left in a peanut butter jar. Add a small amount of boiling water, close jar, and shake. Pour results over bread and flavor with presweetened Kool-Aid.

Dog Food Fried Rice
Virtually identical to what you get for $6.95 in a Chinese restaurant.

Library Paste Guacamole Dip
Made with flour and water. (It tasted great in first grade, didn't it?)

Sandwich Sandwich
A slice of bread between two slices of bread. (If you're short on bread, lay a newspaper on the floor and shake the empty breadbox over it.)

Spice Slumgullion
Seasoning is what gives food its flavor, so if you pour all those little jars of cloves and curry and ginger and garlic salt into boiling water, you should get something delicious.

Air Stew
Use your last $5 to rent an X-rated video and think about something besides food.

do this as any. Pluck the birds until you're tired of getting covered with bloody feathers, then skin them instead. (See if you can get somebody else to do the part where the insides have to be removed. I usually pretend something has gone dangerously wrong with the canoe rack, during this stage of the operation.) Stuff fruit slices in the duck carcass, pour some cheap wine in there and wrap it in foil. Throw this into an oven preheated to 500° and leave it there just long enough to mess up the insides of the stove. The result smells like a drunk tank full of mallards on the Beverly Hills diet.

You can also use fish you've just caught to scare people into not eating. Make the girls clean them. If they won't fall for that, then offer to prepare small-mouth bass sushi with your pocket knife. (Why women think sushi is so keen in Japanese restaurants and so sick-making on a picnic table is one of those mysteries of nature.)

Boat cooking

This is the most elaborate and luxurious method of convincing others that you can cook. Take everybody out on your yacht until they're green in the face. Then you can rave for weeks about your sauce marinara and no one will gainsay you.

If a yacht is too expensive, you can get the same effect in your living room with strobe lights and milk punch.

CHAPTER 5

Entertaining

"That which belongs to another."
—DIOGENES, when asked what wine he liked to drink

O ne of the best things about bachelorhood is that no one expects hospitality from us. We're obviously selfish people or we'd be married and holding up our end of the car pool. Furthermore, society is a free market and we are a scarce commodity. Every hostess in America is wracking her address book for unattached dinner guests.

As long as our looks don't actually gag a cat, we're invited everywhere. In return, all we have to do is keep our fingers out of wedding rings. Ours is the life of the happy drone. The whole hive of civilization is busy feeding us and keeping us amused.

Nevertheless, there are moments when bachelors are expected to act the host. Sometimes lovers or parents corner us, sometimes we give in to misplaced whims of congeniality, and sometimes twenty old S.D.S. buddies show up on the porch, drugged and armed.

There are three types of entertainment a bachelor is traditionally called on to provide:

1. Love trysts
2. Dinner parties
3. Enormous drunken blowouts

Money is your best weapon. Take all your guests to a restaurant and let the restaurant people clean up the mess. If you get someone stupid on the VISA card 800 line, maybe you can convince them that your telephone number is your credit limit. If this fails, try postponing the event in hope of atomic war. Atomic war is much overrated as tragedy, compared to what an enormous drunken blowout can do to your house. If even atomic war fails, follow the directions below.

THE LOVE TRYST

The proper love tryst has three elements:

1. Drinks
2. Cozy meal
3. Interesting excuse

The interesting excuse is not actually interesting. It just gives your date an excuse for not saying goodbye when she ought to. Usually it's a videotape of something high-brow like a Truffaut remake of *Francis Joins the Navy*. With any luck you won't see the end of it.

The important thing in a love tryst it to make your home tug at your date's heartstrings. Women like to think every bachelor is one of the Lost Boys who wandered away from Never-Never Land while Peter and Wendy weren't looking.

Turn your place into a female's idea of a mess, which is to say clean it. Women know we can't take care of ourselves, and they think this is adorable. But that doesn't keep them from blanching at the sight of soap scum. Now muss your home with boyish clutter. Hang neckties from cute places like the refrigerator-door handle. Stick your hat on top of a lampshade. Leave a half-empty wineglass on a table next to a burned-down candle and sheets of stationery covered with crossed-out lines of poetry. (Steal them from Rupert Brooke.) Toss your tuxedo on the floor. And use a wastepaper basket for an ice bucket. This is what women mean when they say, "His place was a fright." If your place is *really* a fright, they won't stay long enough to talk about it.

Be sure all towels and sheets are clean. And make your bed, no matter how strange this seems. Women make their beds each morning and they assume everyone—criminals on the lam, animals in their burrows—does the same. It isn't hard, once you have the knack. Just keep tucking in the end parts of things until their middle parts get smoothed out and flat. But be sure to

Entertaining is less trouble when you trick your guests into helping. Who says too many cooks spoil the ... the ... whatever it is?

move around the bed as you do this. If you stand in one place and tuck, you'll wind up with all the blankets completely under the mattress.

Now wreck dinner. There are two forms of the intentional dinner muff. Using the first method, have all the ingredients for a good dinner ready but don't start cooking until your date arrives. Throw meat that's still wrapped in butcher paper into the oven without a pan. Cram the brown-and-serve rolls into the toaster. As with housecleaning, if you're really incompetent, your date will feel obliged to take over. This, however, is a mean thing to do to a woman, and believe me, she'll know it.

The second method is better. Have the dinner under way before your date arrives, and make sure it's terrifying. Fix baloney soup and pickled beet salad with ouzo and sheep cheese dressing. And make sure all of it, including the salad, catches fire during drinks. Then just when the gruesome slop is supposed to be served, a prearranged pizza delivery boy shows up at the front door.

THE PERFECT LITTLE DINNER PARTY

Why spoil it by showing up? Let people ring your doorbell for a while and go away puzzled but probably relieved. Or be a bully. When you invite your guests, they'll say, "Is there anything I can bring?" Tell them, "Yes, a salad, a vegetable dish, dessert, and an eight-pound standing rib roast—medium rare." Voilà, dinner is served.

If this doesn't work, serve what you can muster and distract like mad. Serve unshucked oysters as hors d'oeuvres. Put the table someplace unusual, like out in the yard in the snow. Dress your dog as a butler. Make guests cook their own live lobsters on weenie forks in the fireplace. If you keep people busy and confused, they're liable to think they're having fun.

THE ENORMOUS DRUNKEN BLOWOUT

Here's an event where bachelor expertise pays off. Bachelors know all about parties. In fact, a good bachelor is a living, breathing party all by himself. At least that is what my girlfriend said when she found the gin bottles under the couch. I believe her exact words were, "You're a disgusting, drunken mess." And that's a good description of a party, if it's done right.

Every society needs to blow off steam. Classical Greece had its Dionysia. Ancient Rome had its bacchanals. But modern America seems to have gotten off the track. We are the only culture to ever develop a type of festivity where you get cornered by a pipe-smoking psych prof who's a bug on nuclear winter.

To turn a dumb soirée into a dangerous bash, the first consideration is time. Don't choose an ordinary time like Saturday night. Have your party at eleven on a weekday morning. The purpose of parties is fun. And *anything* is fun when you're supposed to be working.

A good bachelor is a living, breathing party all by himself.

Other good times for a party are during college exams, jury deliberations, hospital stays, and any time during a marriage.

A good excuse for a party is usually not what you think. Birthdays, weddings, family reunions, and other occasions with an atmosphere of obligatory joy are a bore. Some of the best parties are after funerals. Fun and happiness are not synonymous. Happy people don't need fun. Fun takes your mind off things. If you have a wonderful marriage, beautiful children, a great job, and you're sure you'll go to heaven when you die—why would you want to take your mind off *that?* But the rest of us need lots of fun.

Whatever the occasion, do not neglect alcohol. No other refreshment will do. Yes, alcohol kills brain cells, but it's very selective. It only kills the brain cells that contain good sense, shame, embarrassment, and restraint. Wield a heavy hand at the bar. Spike the white wine. Forget all the soft drinks and most of the mixers; these contain dangerous amounts of water. Water is no fun unless you're throwing people into a swimming pool. You don't want your guests to get *half-*drunk. They might suddenly remember the babysitter, try to drive home, and kill themselves. If a guest is able to make it to the end of your driveway, you've unleashed a dangerous maniac on America's highways.

You also need to have your party in the right kind of place, a place that's too small. You have to pack people together to make them act silly. Try this experiment with house cats. Observe what five house cats do in a living room. Now observe what they do in a laundry sack. This is why parties on boats and in bathtubs are always successful. But any unusual place, regardless of size, is good. High dangerous places like roofs and bridges are excellent. Caves, abandoned warehouses, and beachfront motels during hurricanes are also great. The party spirit responds to any bizarre locale. A bachelor apartment qualifies.

Lots of noise and lots of people are a must for a good party. Make sure some of these people hate each other. Otherwise there will be no chemistry. What would the universe be like if there were only positively charged protons and no negatively charged electrons? Nothing would happen. The most basic molecules couldn't exist. The world wouldn't have hydrogen, let alone cute blond girls in short skirts. Chaos takes organization.

Not every kind of noise will do either. You can't play RUN DMC if you're fêting the Capitol Hill set. To pick the right music, determine your party crowd's median age. Then play hit songs from the most mentally retarded period of their lives—when they were in their teens.

SAMPLE PARTY MUSIC CHOICES

Crowd	Noise
Investment bankers in middle forties	Motown and Beach Boys
Media executives in late thirties	Vanilla Fudge, Captain Beefheart

Crowd	Noise
Bond lawyers in early thirties	Steely Dan, Bee Gees
Out-of-work MBA's in late twenties	Devo, Sex Pistols

One final point: In order to make sure the party gets completely out of hand, you'll need "party catalysts." Drugs are okay, but things for the guests to throw at each other are better, also legal. Have plenty of things available to throw, and if no one takes the hint, throw them yourself—Jell-O cubes, snowballs, wet paper towels. Things that squirt are good, too—seltzer bottles, warm champagne. If that doesn't get things going, bust up the furniture.

CHAPTER 6

Bachelor Decorating

"Off the floor by 40."

— BACHELOR ALAN WELLIKOFF
on the subject of his mattress

*L*eft completely to his own devices, the bachelor's idea of interior decorating is a pyramid of empty beer cans on a window sill.

Bachelors don't live in furnished apartments. We just live in apartments that are furnished like furnished apartments. Whatever was there or was left there or somehow got there, stays there. Forever. A bachelor apartment has more footstools than chairs, a Barcalounger in the kitchen, and a dining-room suite consisting of one stepladder and a card table. The only concessions to art and beauty are nude pictures of

Decorating with Alcohol

1. Start with an empty room and take a big drink.

2. See, it looks better already. Take another drink.

3. Drink a bunch more.

4. Hey, this place looks great, dammit! Know what I mean?
This is a great-looking damn place. Looks great.

Natassia Kinski taped to the bathroom door. If there's a guest room, it has a jet ski and two hundred pounds of fishing tackle in it. And somewhere, probably right where you're going to step in it, is a disassembled motorcycle carburetor in a bucket of gasoline.

There are a lot of inexplicables about a bachelor apartment. Why do I have thirty steak knives and only one teaspoon? What's a dead ficus tree doing in the hall closet? How did the animal tracks get on the ceiling? I don't know. And I don't care. I've got better things to do with my weekends than spend them shopping for wallpaper.

There are just four rules to bachelor decorating:

1. Don't buy anything nice. You're going to wreck it.
2. Don't have wall-to-wall carpet. It's difficult to pick up and take outside to shake. And it's hard to bring along on a picnic.
3. Don't own a waterbed. Lying down drunk on a waterbed is, except for impotence and jail, the worst thing that can happen to a bachelor after midnight.
4. Don't allow yourself to be influenced in any way by mothers, sisters, dates, or women friends. Paint the whole place flat black if you want. Put easy chairs on the roof. Hook up the toilet in the middle of the living room. It's your home and you can do what you want to do.

And what you probably want to do is move.

CHAPTER 7

Home Repair

Lord Finchley tried to mend the Electric Light
Himself. It struck him dead: And serve him right!
It is the business of the wealthy man
To give employment to the artisan.

— HILAIRE BELLOC

House—a construction of wood, bricks, cement, plaster, glass, wiring, and pipes, most of it put together wrong and the rest you're going to ruin when you try to fix it.

There are two kinds of home repair projects: those too big to undertake yourself and those too small to bother with. The first kind you can't afford, and the second kind, if left alone, will develop into something you can't afford either. This is what makes the Mr. Fix-It type so sullen, moping around all Saturday at the lumber yard, clothes full of plaster dust, and thumbs swollen to the size of grapefruits. He should be home getting stewed and watching a ball game like any self-respecting bachelor.

The only household do-it-yourself jobs the average male is equipped to perform are changing light bulbs and building bookcases. If you have some big, tall, thick books and you balance the boards very carefully on top of them, there's nothing to building a bookcase. (The *Time-Life Encyclopedia of Home Repair* is excellent for this.)

CHANGING LIGHT BULBS

Changing light bulbs is not as easy as it sounds. You have to have the right equipment, which in this case is light bulbs. So you go to the store, buy a six-pack, cigarettes, the paper, Cheez Doodles, an auto swap guide, a new Bic, forget the light bulbs, come

---

How-To Tip #1

How to Use a Spirit Level
Place level on any horizontal surface you've just built. Tap vigorously on bubble. Claim that it's wrong.

---

home, and sit in the dark. This is time-consuming, expensive, and ultimately fruitless.

PAINTING

Chief among the home repair projects that normally sensible men attempt is painting. Be sure to buy the easy-to-use water-based latex paint. Though the phrase "easy-to-use" on a home repair product is always a lie. No matter how easy it is to use, it will never be as easy as not using it.

Preparation is vital in painting. Be sure that whatever is going to get paint on it is properly prepared. What's going to get the most paint on it is you. So you'd better have a drink.

Painting is easiest if you paint everything the same color. Pick one shade and stick to it. And cleaning up is easiest if that shade is the same as your skin color. The second-best choice is something that matches whatever you're going to get paint on besides yourself, the couch, for instance. Unfortunately there is no plaid paint. Another idea is to pick a color that will wear well and not show dirt, for example:

Fingerprint gray
Mud
Smudge
Grease beige

The Bachelor's E-Z Guide to Home Appliance Repair

How to fix a toaster

How to fix a can opener

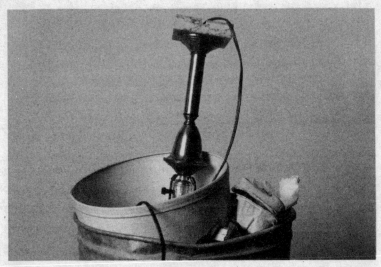

How to fix a lamp

How to fix a television

How-To Tip #2

Finding Electrical Wires in the Wall

You can find electrical wires in the wall by drilling at random with a power drill—this will always hit an electrical wire. (It's also a good way to find water pipes.)

As a rule of thumb, a ceiling should have twice as much paint on it as your hair.

When painting the trim around windows, consider the view. Do you really want to look at it?

Painting techniques that seem like they'd work but don't

- Dipping the dog in paint and letting him shake himself in the middle of the room
- Setting a paint can on the floor and dropping a cherry bomb in it
- Painting trim with a squirt gun

Cleanup

Use the right equipment to clean brushes, rollers, paint trays, etc. I use the garbage can.

Exterior painting

Exterior painting is just like interior painting, except why would you want to paint the exterior? The grass and trees look fine the way they are.

ROOF REPAIRS

Remember, when making roof repairs, the most important thing on the roof is . . . you. If you value your hide, you'll get down from there this minute.

But if you really have to get a TV antenna up or you'll miss the National League playoffs, be sure to do it in a rainstorm. Wherever you're holding the antenna when lightning strikes is the place where it will get the best reception.

All other roof repairs should be done from the safest part of the roof, which is the attic. There are several approaches you can take to fixing roof leaks from the attic, although none of them work. And training the mice to empty buckets and pans will probably take time and patience. Maybe you should move the bed to the first floor.

Home Tool Kit

A Brief List of Tools You Should Have in the Home and What They Are Used For

Screwdriver

For opening beer cans when the pop-top has broken off, stirring paint, getting quarters out of cracks in the floor. Handle may be used as hammer or for tapping stuck jar lids.

Phillips Head Screwdriver

For punching holes in cans of motor oil.

Adjustable Wrench

For pounding nails.

Pliers

For opening greasy tubes of sun block. Use in place of hammer when you can't find the adjustable wrench.

Claw Hammer

For making delicate adjustments to thermostats, storm windows, loose plumbing fixtures and for threatening burglars and pounding screws.

Trowel

For buttering toast when all the knives are dirty.

Wood Chisel

For masonry work, turning screws, spreading grout or roofing tar.

Cross-Cut Saw

For swatting the cat, propping open screen doors.

Tin Snips

For emergency haircuts and detaching drumsticks from roast chickens.

Scotch Tape

For making all actual repairs.

INSULATION

Nevertheless, the attic is an excellent place to install insulation, which conserves heat as well as soaking up some of the water from the roof leaks. Fiberglass is the best insulation material. Fiberglass is expensive but don't try to make your own by putting beer bottles in a leaf shredder.

Rolls of commercial fiberglass should be handled carefully because fiberglass can irritate the skin. Cover your face and limbs, wear gloves, and a hat. When you've got all this on you'll be warm and won't need insulation.

WINDOW REPAIRS

To repair a broken window, cut a piece of glass to size by scoring with a glass cutter. Rap the smaller portion of the scored glass sharply with a screwdriver handle or other blunt instrument. Now go to the hardware store and have a second piece of glass cut to size. This will break while you're bringing it home in the car. Get a third piece of glass and drop this after applying putty to the window frame. Cover the window with a plastic dry-cleaning bag fastened in place with Scotch tape.

HANGING A DOOR

Trim the door to size. Set trimmed door in door frame. Shim all four sides with small wooden wedges and have the door fall right over on top of you. Cover the door with two plastic dry-cleaning bags fastened in place with Scotch tape, and go in and out through the broken window.

WATERPROOFING THE CELLAR

Filling the basement with water will usually keep any ground moisture from seeping in.

FIXING THE FURNACE

Three crucial things to remember about furnaces:

1. Furnaces cannot be started with jumper cables no matter how good the battery is in your car.
2. All furnaces burn something—oil, gas, coal, wood, sometimes the house.
3. Usually what's wrong with the furnace is that whatever it burns, you're out of it. (Make sure you

know what this is. Don't stuff twigs and bark into a fuel-oil tank.)

Furnace repair requires special techniques. A married man normally goes down to the basement, bangs on the steampipes with his shoe, smudges his face slightly, comes upstairs, and tells his wife he doesn't have the right tools, she'd better call a repairman. This doesn't work, however, when you're a bachelor.

BRICKWORK

You can't make bricks without straw, as they say, so first buy some of that. Then again, as far as I can tell, you can't make bricks with straw either. You're going to have to become a mason. I don't know how wearing a fez and learning a secret handshake will help, but it may.

PLUMBING

Leaky faucets

Remove the faucet handle and wash the ceiling. Close the water valve under the sink and try again. Now the faucet handle won't come off. Tie an old dress sock to the mouth of the faucet and stuff the toe in the drain. This will let the water drip without keeping you up all night.

Blocked septic tanks

There must be some kind of fish that would keep everything clean and tidy down there. Very likely it's the fish they use to make Mrs. Paul's Frozen Fish Sticks. Thaw a package of these very slowly at room temperature. Brush the bread crumbs off before flushing them down the toilet.

Do-it-yourself Jacuzzi

Run a garden hose in through the bathroom window.

Other plumbing tasks

Plumbing is easy—if you're a plumber. And if you were a plumber, you'd earn enough to have somebody else doing your home repairs, especially the plumbing.

ELECTRICAL WORK

There are three ways to wire a light switch, two of which will kill you and I forget the other one. The same goes for installing baseboard electrical outlets, but at least it's less of a fall to the floor when you drop dead.

You can avoid the problem of light switches and outlets altogether if you have a dozen extension cords dangling from the overhead fixture. This also gives you something to grab onto when you're drunk and can't get out of your chair.

FLOOR REFINISHING

Refinishing floors is nonsense. Floors are either finished or they aren't. If you can see into the basement, the floor isn't finished.

Laying linoleum

Cut the sheet of linoleum to the shape of the room. Then lay it down on the floor. It will look better and be less lumpy if you remove the furniture first.

Laying wall-to-wall carpet

You can lay wall-to-wall carpet yourself or you can take the carpet you have already and adjust the walls accordingly.

REPLASTERING WALLS

Small holes in the wall can be repaired by putting something in front of them, the landlord, for example. Put the landlord right in front of the hole and tell him, "Do you think I'm going to pay rent for a place with holes in the wall?" If it's your own home, use a bookcase, or a poster of Cindy Crawford.

Sheetrocking

Sheetrock is actually a layer of gypsum compound placed between two pieces of paper, a sort of plaster sandwich. It's lousy to eat, and if you try to put it up yourself, the walls will look about like a picnic basket.

Picture hanging

Taping pictures directly to the wall saves framing expenses.

INSTALLING SMOKE DETECTORS

Smoke detectors come with simple installation instructions. Insert batteries and place smoke detector as directed. Now light a cigar. *Bzzzzzzzzzzzzzzzz.* Build a fire in the fireplace. *Bzzzzzzzzzzzzzzzz.* Try to cook dinner. *Bzzzzzzzzzzzzzzzz.* Remove batteries and give the smoke detector to the dog to play with.

CHAPTER 8

Yard Care

The world would be a better place if it was half-dark, indoors, and air-conditioned.

— LARRY L. KING

*I*f your home has a front yard, you may be wondering what's it doing out there? A good question, since there's no record that the ancient Vikings, Mongol hordes, Oglala Sioux, or any other civilization that bachelors admire had front yards. That lawn is a pathetic suburban imitation of the pasture land or park surrounding an eighteenth-century English manor house. Since you don't graze sheep in the flower beds or course deer down the driveway with greyhounds, you may find this silly.

It is. The whole idea of yard care is silly. Man has

only been on this planet for about a million years. Who took care of the yard before we were around? And we're ruining the one really good thing about nature, that it never needs to be dusted, swept, or taken to the dry cleaner. Plus the most interesting kind of women regard the outdoors as something the cat dragged in, so it's no use having a lawn on their account.

For those of you who haven't looked lately, there are three kinds of plants growing in a yard:

GRASS—the low, green stuff
SHRUBBERY—grass that *really* needs to be mowed
TREES—Shrubbery that has grown out of control

And who wouldn't rather live in a forest than a sub-development? Just *let* the damn lawn go. This is the natural and organic thing to do anyway.

Unfortunately, there are some reasons for keeping the yard nice. Maybe you're having an affair with your next-door neighbor's wife. You don't want to give him *two* things to complain about. Maybe you want to keep an area clear for games of touch football with the local cocktail waitresses—shirts *vs.* skins. And when you don't mow, it can be hard to find those cars you've got up on blocks in the front yard. Plus there's hunting. Even if you don't course with greyhounds, you still might want to put a salt lick out by the birdbath to attract deer. And, if there's a head-high tangle of under-brush in the way, you're not going to get a clear shot at that ten-point buck from your bedroom window.

Herewith, a quick guide to low-effort yard care.

LAWNS

Mowing is tedious and can be avoided by wetting down the yard with a fine spray of #2 heating oil. Or during the winter months you can sprinkle rock salt on the whole thing.

If you prefer a live lawn, cultivate crabgrass. It is low and spreading and doesn't need to be cut as often as the regular kind. It also dies off quicker in the fall. I'm not sure exactly how to cultivate crabgrass. The seeds don't seem to be sold in garden centers. But whatever it is I do to my own lawn works pretty well. What I do is as little as possible.

When you finally do have to cut the grass, make it bearable with frequent beer breaks and extensive fantasies. Each of those blades of grass is a member of "Beverly Hills 90210." There goes Luke Perry's head. Trouble is, he's the only one whose name I can remember. How about talk-show hosts—Donahue all over the place, Oprah next, then Arsenio Hall.

Or the power mower is a gigantic, all-terrain logging machine clearing the rain forest in the Amazon basin for Jack Bachelor, world's richest man, whose million-acre plantation will grow beautiful young women. One of them has just bought the house next door—the neighbors and their kids having made a sudden emergency move to Cleveland. She's independently wealthy, looks like Daryl Hannah and comes over while you're mowing the lawn. "Do you have any spare baby oil?" she says, wearing nothing but high-heel shoes.

An "organic" or "natural-style" lawn is maintenance-free and doesn't look any worse than the rest of the outdoors.

When you're finished running the lawn mower over your foot and gotten out of the hospital, give a local kid five bucks and the keys to the Toro.

FLOWERS

You can get flowers at the dime store in a variety of colors. They're made out of plastic, and they last for years.

VEGETABLE GARDENING

The only kind of vegetable gardening real bachelors do is with pot plants and Grow Lights in the closet. Consult your old hippie friends from college.

GETTING READY FOR WINTER

You can rake leaves into a pile and burn them or you can just burn them. Which is easier? Which is more fun? Squirt charcoal lighter around the yard, get on the other side of your neighbor's fence, and toss a match.

It's all right to put off mowing the lawn, but don't put it off until February.

PRUNING, MULCHING, GRAFTING, PLANTING, WEEDING, CLIPPING, THINNING, COMPOSTING, CULTIVATING, SEEDING, LANDSCAPING, LIMING, DIGGING, ROLLING, HOEING, FERTILIZING, CONTROLLING APHIDS AND CUTWORMS, AND TRIMMING ALONG THE EDGES OF THE SIDEWALK

Hah! Who's going to make you? Roll over and go back to sleep. You're not married.

CHAPTER 9

Children Are Bachelors, Too, More or Less

(Witches) steal young children out of their cradles ... and put deformed in their rooms, which we call changelings.

—ROBERT BURTON

Or kids that our girlfriend has from her first marriage.

—ANONYMOUS BACHELOR

$\mathcal{S}$ome bachelors have children, either by ex-wives or by accident, and all bachelors are subjected to them occasionally. It pays to know how to handle the things. I've been making a study of the subject and have reached two principal conclusions. One is that there's a lot of nonsense talked about "people who treat their children like beasts." Treating children like beasts, especially like dogs, is perfectly reasonable. You pat their heads, scratch them behind the ears. Give them simple meals in unbreakable dishes. (Child food is very similar to dog food. I defy you to tell the difference between Spaghetti-O's and Kibbles and Bits.) And you housebreak them.

You speak to a child in the same tone of voice you speak to a dog, and you say almost the same things to both of them. "Good boy." "Down, boy." "Sit." All bachelors love dogs, and we would love children just as much if they could be taught to retrieve.

My second conclusion is that everybody knows how to raise children, except the people who have them. I don't have any children, but when my friends' kids are running around like Apaches and turning the household breakables into landfill, I always have good advice. (There is such a thing as military preschool, isn't there?)

TIPS ON HANDLING CHILDREN
OF VARIOUS AGES

Birth to age four

Getting down on all fours and imitating a rhinoceros stops babies from crying. (Put an empty cigarette pack on your nose for a horn and make loud "snort" noises.) I don't know why parents don't do this more. Usually it makes the kid laugh. Sometimes it sends him into shock. Either way it quiets him down. If you're a parent, acting like a rhino has another advantage. Keep it up until the kid is a teenager and he definitely won't have his friends hanging around your house all the time.

Age two to four

For toddlers I suggest leaving their mittens on year-round, indoors and out. That way they can't get into aspirin bottles, liquor cabinets, or boxes of kitchen matches. Also, it keeps their little hands clean for meal-times. Better yet, leave the whole snowsuit on. This slows them up and keeps them from hurting themselves when they fall over. In fact, if it's one of those really bulky snowsuits, they *can't* fall over.

Age five to ten

Children from the age of five to ten should watch more television. Television depicts adults as rotten SOB's, given to fistfights, gunplay, and other mayhem. Kids who believe this about grownups aren't likely to argue about bedtime. They know what happens to people who argue about bedtime with Hulk Hogan. Also, kids who watch TV learn that adults settle many of their quarrels with car chases. Kids aren't stupid. They know they can't reach the pedals and see over the dashboard at the same time.

Age eleven to twenty-five

Older children should be taught responsibility. Give them something to look after, take care of, and feel affection for. How about the kitchen? Even better, how about the kitchen at my house? I've always thought the best part of the Cinderella story was how the wicked stepfolk never had to clean month-old linguine out of the bottom of a pot.

TIPS ON THE HANDLING OF MOTHERS AND FATHERS OF CHILDREN

The truth is, bachelors see things from the child's point of view. We don't have children around all the time to cloud our memories of childhood. We pretend to be mystified by kids, but what we're really mystified by is moms and dads. We didn't understand them thirty years ago, and we don't understand them now.

There's something about getting married and having children that turns ordinary people into . . . parents. Here's a young man and a young woman who have been putting their feet up on furniture all their lives. They have one child, and suddenly feet on the furniture is a

Trick-or-Treat hint for kids: If you really want to scare a bachelor on Halloween, dress up as a child—his child.

crime worse than arson. Many of us have stayed single well into middle life for fear that if we ever got married and had children we'd start making everybody, including ourselves, eat lima beans.

There's probably some logic to parental behavior, but the bachelor can't fathom it. Why drag a four-year-old to the grocery store and then swat him for being bored? The grocery store bores me, and if I went there more often, I'd howl bloody murder myself. On the other hand, I've seen more than one kid caught torturing the poodle and given nothing but a dull lecture on the House Pet Bill of Rights.

Then there's the "No!" blizzard that follows small children everywhere. Personally, I'd just let Junior nibble on things in the ashtray. He won't do it twice. But then parents turn right around and let their children do anything, let six-year-olds call me by my first name and get jelly all over my Helmut Newton photography books.

As far as I can tell, all children are both spoiled and pestered silly about every little thing they do. This is why there are two things a bachelor hates to see: Children being spanked. And children not being spanked.

THE REAL TRUTH ABOUT CHILDREN

The real truth about children is they don't speak the language very well. They're physically uncoordinat-

ed. And they are ignorant of our elaborate ideas about
right and wrong. The kindly bachelor thinks, "We'd be
more understanding with an adult who was a foreigner
or hopelessly clumsy or from another planet." But
would we really be more understanding with an all-
thumbs extra-terrestrial who spoke nothing but French
and didn't know the golden retriever puppy wasn't supposed to go in the washing machine? And what if he
came to live with us for eighteen years?

CHAPTER 10

Miscellaneous Bachelor
Hints and Tips

You are pictures out of doors,
Bells in your parlors, wildcats in your kitchens . . .
Players in your housewifery,
  and housewives in your beds.
—WILLIAM SHAKESPEARE, OTHELLO, ACT II, SCENE 1

CAR CARE

End car-care worries forever by parking the thing
in Manhattan with the windows down and the keys in
the ignition.

CHRISTMAS DECORATIONS

Real bachelors do not feel the urge to put up Christmas decorations. Except sometimes when they get very drunk and sentimental on Christmas Eve. If this happens to you, paint your behind red and green and press it against the front window.

DESIGNING YOUR OWN HOME

If you ever get the chance to have a house built to your specifications, here are several ideas you might keep in mind:

- Cement floors with central drains in every room will facilitate cleaning, especially if combined with waterproof walls and belongings. Put exterior-style garden-hose faucets along the baseboards.
- Install a commercial sprinkler system if you smoke and tend to doze off in armchairs. Sprinkler systems are also useful for quick showers during breakfast when you're late for work.
- Put a built-in exhaust fan in every room. This lets you put off emptying ashtrays.
- Plumb the whole house with plastic tubing for beer taps.
- Make sure you have one cable hook-up for every major sports event that might be on TV simultaneously.

The toilet is a handy place for pet baths. Squirt liquid dish soap in toilet bowl and insert pet. Flush once for cats, hamsters, or guinea pigs, twice for dogs.

- Hide the outlet in the bathroom. Put it behind the athlete's foot powder in the medicine chest, so you can use it for your electric razor but your date can't find it for her hair dryer. This will keep the bathroom from being tied up for hours.

ENERGY-WASTING TIPS

Use these if you hate your landlord and utility charges are included in your rent.

- Turn the hot-water heater all the way up so you can steam lobsters in the shower.
- Shovel the driveway with the electric stove. Turn the broiler on, lay the stove face down, and drag it back and forth across the snow.

HALLOWEEN

Be sure to remember when Halloween is. Answering the door when you're three-quarters crocked and finding a pack of midget He-Man, Master of the Universes, on the front porch can be a scary experience if you're not expecting it.

HOME FINANCE

You can't put your VISA bill on your American Express card.

HOUSEHOLD CLEANING PRODUCTS

Avoid all home cleaning products that claim to be effective against grease. Grease is slippery and keeps dirt from adhering to kitchen appliances, dishes, and glassware.

INSURANCE

Does your homeowner's insurance give you full coverage for the following types of bachelor liabilities?

- Indoor car accidents
- Bedsheet grease fires
- Damage to wildlife from massive liquor spills
- Dinner guests stuck in the chimney
- Dirt tornados
- Explosions while playing with the microwave
- Electrical blackouts during important sports events
- Your cooking

No home should be without a complete first-aid kit.

- Large wagers placed on the Cleveland Indians while drunk
- Living-room dog polo injuries

LAUNDRY AND DRY-CLEANING TIPS

- You can dry-clean your clothes at home by dipping them in gasoline. (Clothes will be permanently free of all dirt if you do this near an open flame.)
- Gasoline smell can be removed from clothes by sending them to the dry cleaner.
- Press wrinkled trousers by putting them between the mattress and box spring before going to bed drunk. In the morning you'll frantically search the house for your pants, and when you finally remember they're between the mattress and the box spring, you'll be so happy to find them you won't care that they're wrinkled.
- An alternative to wearing your clothes in the bathtub is to bathe in the washing machine. Either technique saves hot water. Watch out for that agitator thing.
- If the local laundry repeatedly loses your shirts, you may want to try the traditional Third World method of dealing with laundry, which is to have your laundry man beaten on rocks.
- Ronald E. Burr, publisher of *The American Spectator*, writes in with this tip: "If you buy 121 2/3 pairs of boxer shorts, you'll only have to go to the laundromat three times a year."

NEW USES FOR DIRTY LAUNDRY

Executive-length dress sock:
- dog collar
- sweat band
- blackjack (put roll of quarters in the toe)
- thermos cozy
- shoe buffer
- stuff it with crumpled newspapers to stop drafts under doors
- tie it around your arm to show you're in mourning

White wool sweat sock:
- mitten
- tub stopper
- potholder
- mood enhancer (stuck on top of a bare light bulb)

Boxer shorts:
- party hat

PET NAMING

One of the great pleasures of bachelorhood is naming the dog. Married men have to let their children do it, and as a result often find themselves in the hunting field, yelling, "Fluffy! Fluffy!" or "Heel, Puff, heel!"

Here are some decent red-blooded things to call your dog:

Regular checking, NOW account, or tinder in the fireplace? Setting fire to money can be an excellent alternative, considering how much trouble bachelors get into whenever they have cash.

CIVIL WAR GENERALS
(North of Maryland)
Grant
Sherman
(South of Pennsylvania)
Stonewall
Lee

FAVORITE PRESIDENTS
Ike
Cal
Hoover
Teddy

DOG IN ANOTHER LANGUAGE
Pero—Spanish
Kleb—Arabic
Hund—German
Dinner—Vietnamese

SPORTS FIGURES
Babe
Ty
Leon
Olga

HISTORICAL FIGURES
Genghis
Attila
Rommel
Stalin
Herod

MISC.
Harley
Vette
Skull
Hiroshima

And don't forget the names of old girlfriends, your present girlfriend's nickname, teachers you had in grade school, and the first names of your parents.

If you have a cat, you shouldn't name it at all. You can't call a cat.

PEST CONTROL

Cockroaches

Cockroaches have been given a bad rap. They don't bite, smell, or get into your booze. Would that all houseguests were as well behaved. The ancient Egyptians even venerated the cockroach as a symbol of the sun. Well, actually, that was the scarab beetle, but worship one bug, and you'll worship them all.

Don't do anything about cockroaches. There's nothing you *can* do anyway.

Mice

Don't put cheese in a mousetrap. Mice are much more attracted to fat, suet, peanut butter, and book bindings. And if you examine this list, you'll see that, if the mice got it, you probably didn't want it anyway. So don't do anything about the mice either.

Rats

Rats are another matter. You have to do something about rats. But don't poison them because they'll die in the walls. And a dead rat in the wall is the one thing on earth that can, I guarantee, make your bachelor home more disgusting than it is now.

*Is this kind of thing covered by your homeowner's policy?
Check with your insurance agent today.*

I once lived in a house that had rats. I took a handful of diet pills and sat up all night with a bottle of whiskey and a pistol waiting for them to poke their heads out of the woodwork. By four A.M. I was seeing any number of rats, many of them Day-Glo orange and wearing ballet costumes. This technique is not very effective.

Traps are not very effective either. If you check on your rat traps in the middle of the night, you're liable to see the rats using them as Nautilus machines.

However, while researching this book I came across another method of getting rid of rats. It appears in a volume called *Household Discoveries, Encyclopedia of Practical Recipes and Processes,* by Sidney Morse, published in 1913. I have no idea if this works, but it does sound like fun:

> Catch one or more rats in a wire cage. Take a pronged stick . . . wedge the fork just behind the animal's ears, and pin him firmly to the floor. . . . Roll a bit of newspaper into a tight cylinder, set fire to one end and with the lighted end singe the hair from his back. . . . Fix a small paintbrush on a long stick . . . apply a coating of phosphoric mixture, slightly warm, to the animal's back, and release him near his hole. Just what impression is produced by what seems to be the ghost of a departed rat reappearing in his old haunts would be hard to say, but those who have tried the experiment report that no rats remain in the vicinity to give an account of their sentiments.

SEWING ON BUTTONS

Don't. You should always be missing some buttons. It's part of your boyish bachelor charm. Many a woman has sat down on the living-room couch to sew on a button and has wound up doing something more interesting on another piece of furniture elsewhere in the home.

If, however, you're involved with one of those very modern young women who prides herself on being useless around the house, you can reattach buttons with a stapler.

SNOW AND ICE REMOVAL

Snow shoveling can be avoided by running your car up and down the sidewalk, packing the snow down and making it easy to walk on.

UPHOLSTERY CLEANING

There's no way to get a chair into the washing machine or even the shower stall. Upholstery cannot be cleaned. The best thing to do is cover the furniture with something such as the skin of a wild animal, a blonde, for instance.

Taking clothes off before getting into shower or tub adds unnecessary steps to maintaining personal hygiene.

BACHELOR'S HALL

Bachelor's Hall, what a comical place it is!
Keep me from such all the days of my life!
Sure but he knows what a burning disgrace it is,
Never at all to be getting a wife.

Pots, dishes, and pans, and such other commodities,
Ashes and praty-skins, kiver the floor;
His cupboard a storehouse of comical oddities,
Things never thought of as neighbors before.

When his meal it is over with, the table's left
   sittin' so,
Dishes, take care of yourselves if you can;
Devil a drop of hot water will visit ye.
Och, let him alone for a baste of a man!

Late in the night, when he goes to bed shivering,
Never the bit is his bed made at all;
So he creeps like a terrapin under the kivering;—
Bad luck to the pictur of Bachelor's Hall!
   —ANONYMOUS (collected by William Cullen Bryant,
                    Library of World Poetry, 1870)